AIDS:

WHAT EVERY RESPONSIBLE

CANADIAN SHOULD KNOW

AIDS:

WHAT EVERY RESPONSIBLE

CANADIAN SHOULD KNOW

Canadian Cataloguing in Publication Data
Greig, James (James Douglas), 1942-
    AIDS: What Every Responsible Canadian Should Know

Co-published with: Canadian Public Health Association
Includes index.
Bibliography
ISBN 920197-46-9

1. AIDS (disease) - Popular works
I. Canadian Public Health Association
II. Title.

RC607.A26G74 1987 616.9'792 C87-090139-7

Published by Summerhill Press
and
The Canadian Public Health Association
1565 Carling Avenue, Suite 400
Ottawa, Ontario K1Z 8R1

Distributed by the University of Toronto Press
5201 Dufferin Street, Downsview, Ontario M3H 5T8

Printed in Canada

About the author

James D. Greig has been a public relations and marketing consultant for over twenty years, specializing in corporate media relations and political campaigns. He is a freelance feature writer and has written numerous articles for newspapers, trade journals and other publications. He currently resides in Scarborough, Ontario and has recently co-authored a Teacher's Guide to accompany this book. He is also the author of the syndicated newspaper column "AIDS Awareness", published in over 60 newspapers across Canada.

His next book is entitled *Cocaine and Other Drugs: What Every Responsible Canadian Should Know*, and is scheduled to be published early in 1988.

Acknowledgements

The publishers gratefully acknowledge the assistance and material provided by the Federal Centre for AIDS, Ottawa, Ontario, the Atlanta Centers for Disease Control, Atlanta, Georgia, and the World Health Organization (WHO).

Much of this book has been compiled from existing material originally produced by the Ontario Public Education Panel on AIDS (OPEPA) with advice from the Provincial Advisory Committee on AIDS, the Ontario Human Rights Commission, the Ontario Federation of Labour and the InterMinisterial Working Group on AIDS.

Assistance and additional material was also provided by:

Greg Smith
Executive Director
Federal Centre for AIDS
Health and Welfare Canada

Jane Stewart
Communications Officer
Ontario Ministry of Health

D. Sturtevant
Program Officer
Health Promotion Directorate
Health and Welfare Canada

Ann Bowlby
Project Consultant
Ontario Public Education
    Panel on AIDS (OPEPA)

Barbara Jones
Chief, Communications and
    Education Services
Federal Centre for AIDS
Health and Welfare Canada

Anne Moon
Senior Communications
    Officer
City of Toronto Department of
    Public Health

Allan Bierbrier
Associate Executive Director
Canadian Public Health
    Association

Stephen Manning
Executive Director
AIDS Committee of Toronto

Phil Shaw
Communications Director
AIDS Committee of Toronto

Matt Kuefler
Archivist
AIDS Network of Edmonton

Barry G. Breau
Executive Director
AIDS Network of Edmonton

Tracey Tremayne-Lloyd
Chairperson
Health Law Section
Canadian Bar Association

Marion Marks
Kingston AIDS Project

Santo Caira
Provincial AIDS Coordinator
Canadian Haemophilia Society
Ontario Chapter

Dr. Alastair Clayton
Director General
Federal Centre for AIDS
Health and Welfare Canada

Charles Black
V-P Insurance Operations
Canadian Life and Health
  Insurance Association

Kate Wardrop
Health Promotion
  Coordinator
Canadian Public Health
  Association

Dr. John Hardie
Chief
Department of Dentistry
Ottawa Civic Hospital

Alex Berry
Executive Director
Hamilton AIDS Network for
  Dialogue and Support

Ernest A. Dyck
Tsubouchi & Parker
Barristers and Solicitors

Gordon Youngman
Chairman
AIDS Committee of
  Cambridge, Kitchener,
  Waterloo and Area

Kevin Brown
Vancouver Persons with AIDS
(PWA) Coalition

Dr. Ian Gemmill
Associate Medical Officer
  of Health
Ottawa Carleton Regional
  Health Unit

7

Reference material
used to compile this book includes:

- [ ] selected editorial pieces published by all Toronto newspapers
- [ ] various brochures and pamphlets produced by the AIDS Committees throughout Canada
- [ ] Newsweek, Nov. '86
- [ ] John Hopkins Magazine, Dec. '86
- [ ] AIDS Medical Guide published by the San Francisco AIDS Foundation
- [ ] Nature Vol. 324, Nov. '86
- [ ] Facts on AIDS (For the Public) published by The Canadian Public Health Association and written by Elizabeth DePaul and Miriam Liberman
- [ ] The AIDS Phenomenon (A Medical Mystery) published by The Toronto Sun Publishing Corporation and written by Greg Parent
- [ ] Safe Sex in the Age of AIDS prepared by The Institute for Advanced Study of Human Sexuality and published by Citadel Press

Illustrations provided by:

- [ ] Federal Centre for AIDS, Health and Welfare Canada, Ottawa
- [ ] Centers for Disease Control, Atlanta
- [ ] World Health Organization

INTRODUCTION

In many ways, the new epidemic of AIDS has become the ultimate challenge to public health. In five years, it has grown from a trickle of rare illnesses with no known cause or even a name, to become a tidal wave of disease that has shocked us all.

The importance of this book and, in general, public education about AIDS, cannot be overstated. We are still in the first phase of the epidemic which is spreading rapidly throughout the world. It will take years to develop effective medical treatments and vaccines, and mount a global program that will effectively contain the disease. In the meantime, we must put Prevention Through Education in the forefront of the attack on AIDS. This educational effort, to be effective, must be broadly based, not only utilizing the mass media, the schools and the workplace, but also devising innovative local community programs that reach special groups and individuals at risk. A concerted effort by all of us to improve our knowledge, to adopt attitudes of serious concern, and to act with constructive behavior, will stem the tide.

What are some of the main problems to be faced in the prevention of AIDS and how can you help yourself and others to avoid infection?

Fighting fear with the facts

As the virus causing AIDS, the Human Immunodeficiency Virus (HIV), has spread to more people and different groups, our concern as a society has grown. AIDS can no longer be seen as a problem exclusive to small minority groups. So, too, has our understanding of the infection grown. The character of the virus and the way in which it can be spread or alternatively avoided is now much clearer.

Armed with this new knowledge, as outlined in this book, we can identify the real risks, and be reassured rather than fearful, as AIDS is not "caught" in most everyday situations but only as a result of certain "risk behaviors".

Knowledge, then, helps us to control our fear and channel serious concern into behaviors that are AIDS avoiding.

Dealing with tough subjects to talk about:
Sex and drugs

Most Canadians recognize the need for frank discussion and education, about AIDS and the spread of the virus mainly by sex and secondarily by needle sharing for drug abuse. Recent opinion surveys by the Canadian Public Health Association and some provincial agencies have shown 80 to 90% of parents and teenagers in favor of sex education programs in schools, dealing with sexual development, sexually transmitted diseases and disease prevention methods, such as condoms, at a junior and senior high school level.

However, when it comes to actually supporting those who make public health announcements, or school officials who could teach these programs, the will of the majority is often stopped by the complaints of a vocal minority who claim education will promote casual sex. This is not a new argument as it has always been used to oppose sex education, even before contraceptives were introduced.

11

It now appears that the issue of AIDS has aroused such public concern that previous reluctance to provide these necessary programs will be swept away at last. After all, to provide information that can control a major threat to public health and preserve life is one of society's highest responsibilities. Material that seemed too controversial and sensitive to deal with in the media, schools, and public discussion, must now become commonplace.

Understanding rather than denying the risks

A major attitude problem for many of us is the "it can't happen to me" syndrome. This denial of the risks is very commonly expressed by heterosexual men and women who still think this epidemic almost always affects gay men, and that the number affected in Canada is still small.

However, up to 15% of the AIDS disease in Canada, and a higher percentage in the United States, occurs in heterosexual men and women. The time has come for us all to clearly understand that the epidemic is not limited by sexual orientation. Furthermore, we must come to grips with the size of the epidemic. The number of people with AIDS is now around 1700 in Canada, but the best estimate of people with the HIV infection is 30–50,000. It is everyone's responsibility to understand this risk, strengthen their preventative behaviors, and avoid risk behaviors, so that the 50,000 will not grow to 100,000 or 200,000.

Helping rather than blaming

As any epidemic develops, some people, because of where they live or what they do, are affected first or more than others. Very often they are taken by surprise and suffer illness before health authorities can identify the cause and take measures to help those affected and protect the rest of the community. It is not appropriate to blame those involved early for the spread that follows.

It is important to realize that those affected by HIV infection, or people with AIDS, are fighting a life and death battle. They need help in difficult life-long adjustments, and support and care through sometimes devastating illnesses. If others can cope with the fears of the disease and modify lingering prejudices or moral positions about sexual behavior, it will be very important to the quality of life and health of those affected.

Again, an effort to strengthen support and compassion, and forego blaming and moralizing, is needed to deal effectively with the epidemic and the very personal and human needs of those affected and those at risk.

These are but a few of the problems that this book can help us with. In reading it, you will recognize that concerted action is required by all of us *now*, to prevent the further spread of this epidemic. In working with the facts presented here, you can become part of the solution. You can Join the Attack on AIDS!

David J. Walters, M.A., M.D.

Director, AIDS Education and Awareness Program
Canadian Public Health Association
March 1988

Author's note...

This book has been compiled to complement the efforts of the federal and provincial governments, their AIDS advisory committees, local AIDS committees throughout Canada, public health and medical workers, and the thousands of volunteers engaged int he fight against AIDS. *AIDS: What Every Responsible Canadian Should Know* is dedicated to their efforts.

The need for comprehensive information on AIDS is great if our country is to avert what has the potential to become a major epidemic and national crisis. This book becomes one more vehicle to provide that information to the general public. In instances where facts cannot be ascertained, opinions from qualified professionals are noted. These sources are acknowledged.

As you will learn through reading the enclosed material, the greatest threat of AIDS is the rapidly spreading virus which causes it, and can be carried and transmitted by obviously healthy individuals. Herein lies the deadliness of the disease. Only an informed community acting in a responsible manner will be able to keep the AIDS virus in check until a cure or vaccine is discovered.

This book is simply written and designed for easy reading and convenient reference. While certain parts of the book may appear to be repetitive, this is to ensure that those readers who may only be interested in a specific section of the book receive the full benefits of the pertinent information contained on these pages.

The first series of questions are the result of the author's survey concerning the most commonly asked questions about AIDS. While the survey resulted in a compilation of one hundred and forty actual questions, all are answered within the material contained in this book.

It should also be noted that *AIDS: What Every Responsible Canadian Should Know*, is under copyright. However, much of the information herein has been obtained from a variety of sources who have granted permission for the reproduction of their material. It is the desire of all concerned with this publication that all or any part of this book may be used for educational purposes, with the author's written consent, and any activity in that respect is encouraged.

I gratefully acknowledge the assistance and material provided by the Federal Centre for AIDS, Ottawa, Ontario, the Atlanta Center for Disease Control, Atlanta, Georgia, the World Health Organization (WHO), and the Canadian Public Health Association, who not only provided a great deal of the most current information, but carefully scrutinized the manuscript prior to publication.

Finally, while the statistical information contained in this book will have changed to some extent by the time of its eventual publication, the general information provided should not. In the event you are unable to find the answer to any question you might have concerning AIDS in this book you are encouraged to call your local Department of Health or any of the AIDS Committees, or AIDS Advisory Boards listed on pages 131–135.

Good reading... good health,   **James D. Greig**

Contents

THE MOST COMMONLY ASKED QUESTIONS ABOUT AIDS

16

AIDS TESTING

AIDS AND SAFER SEX

AIDS AND GOVERNMENT

AIDS AND WOMEN

INFORMATION FOR PARENTS AND TEACHERS

AIDS AND THE WORKPLACE

AIDS AND DENTISTRY

AIDS AND THE HEALTH CARE WORKER

AIDS AND YOU

THE MOST COMMONLY ASKED

QUESTIONS ABOUT AIDS

What is AIDS?

AIDS (Acquired Immunodeficiency Syndrome) is caused by a virus that attacks the body's immune system, leading to its collapse and thus leaving the person vulnerable to a number of infections or cancers. These infections or cancers are very unusual in anyone whose immune system is working normally. But when they occur in a person as a result of the AIDS virus, he is said to have AIDS. AIDS is really the most advanced stage of disease caused by this virus.

This virus which causes AIDS is found primarily in the blood, semen or vaginal fluid of an infected person, and is spread when any of these substances enters another person's body (bloodstream).

The virus has also been isolated in the laboratory from tears and saliva of some infected individuals. However, in over 80,000 known cases of AIDS worldwide, not one is known to have contracted the disease from these body fluids.

What causes AIDS?

AIDS is caused by a virus that has been given various names by different groups of researchers: Human T-lymphotropic virus, type III (HTLV-III); lymphadenopathy associated virus (LAV); or AIDS-related virus (ARV). Internationally, it is most commonly called the **Human Immunodeficiency Virus (HIV)**. (HIV will be the term used throughout the remainder of this book).

If this virus gets into the bloodstream, it infects and destroys white blood cells called helper-T cells. These white blood cells are very important to the body's immune system because they help direct the fight against disease. Once the cells are infected, the immune system cannot function properly.

Infection with this virus does not always lead to AIDS, and researchers are investigating whether other co-factors may be necessary to trigger the disease. However, even though some people infected with HIV may appear to remain in good health for a long time, it is not yet known how many people will go on to develop illnesses, some fatal, in the years to come.

In 1986, the U.S. National Academy of Science estimated that between 25 to 50 percent of those infected with the virus will develop AIDS eventually. The Centers for Disease Control in Atlanta estimate that between 10 to 30 percent of those infected will go on to the final stages of AIDS within the next five to ten years. Several studies of groups of HIV infected men have shown that 35% develop AIDS by seven years, the longest any group has been studied.

As more groups are studied over a longer period of time, this issue will be clarified. Presently we can only say that an increasing number of people who are infected go on to fully develop AIDS with time.

How did AIDS originate?

Because there is still so much to be learned about AIDS, the origin of the virus is debatable. Some scientists believe that HIV is a constantly mutating virus that has existed for generations and its properties have only recently been altered, causing it to become fatal. In the United States, AIDS was first diagnosed and recorded in 1981, although there is evidence of the disease as far back as 1979. In Canada, the first case of AIDS was diagnosed in 1982.

The most popular theory is that AIDS originated in Africa, where it is speculated that the disease may have been transmitted to man from monkeys. Blood tests conducted on two hundred African green monkeys at Harvard University found that seventy percent of them were infected with a virus not dissimilar to HIV, but distinctly different in disease potential from the virus that causes AIDS in humans.

The first documented cases of AIDS started to appear in the mid-1970s in central Africa. In 1960, Zaire (formerly the Belgian Congo) declared its independence and began a massive rebuilding and restructuring program supported by the United Nations. The UN offered three and six year employment contracts to French speaking professionals, including teachers and technicians from nations such as France, Belgium and Haiti. Although many did not return to their homelands following their employment contract in Zaire, it is believed that some who did may have brought HIV with them, to Europe, the Caribbean and North America.

Haiti has been particularly hard hit, with 912 cases, one of the highest rates per capita in the world. Haiti, a popular vacation island in the Caribbean, attracts thousands of North American tourists each year, which suggests some may have practised risk behaviors while on vacation and brought the infection back to the United States and Canada.

How serious is the AIDS epidemic?

AIDS is a world-wide phenomenon. In addition to Canada and the United States, AIDS has been reported to the World Health Organization (WHO) from 129 countries throughout the Americas, Europe, Africa and Australia. The Middle East and Asia are also beginning to report some cases.

The World Health Organization (WHO) now estimates that there are at least 150,000 cases worldwide, and five to ten million are infected with HIV.

In Canada there are 1622 cases, of whom 886 have died (March 7, 1988).

WHO predicts that by 1991 there will be from 500,000 to 3 million people with AIDS and that up to 100 million people could be infected with HIV. It cannot be estimated at this time how many of these people will go on to develop AIDS or ARC (AIDS-related complex).

There have been 54,233 confirmed cases of AIDS recorded in the United States since 1981 and it is estimated that by 1991 there will have been 270,000 cases reported.

It is estimated that up to 50,000 Canadians and 1.5 million Americans have been exposed to HIV. These are the carriers of the virus, and they are considered capable of transmitting it through sexual activity, sharing drug needles or other specific risk behaviors.

WHO has reported that AIDS is spreading rapidly in South and Central America, Africa, and is moving into the populous regions of Asia. Specific numbers of cases in many of these areas cannot be determined because it is believed that thousands of cases may not have been diagnosed as AIDS and have gone unreported (this is particularly true in the African nations).

As of February 1, 1988, the World Health Organization has reported the following number of AIDS cases in this selection of countries:

Country or region	Total AIDS Cases
Canada	1,622
United States	54,233
Total North America	**55,855**
Brazil	2,485
Dominican Republic	352
Haiti	912
Mexico	713
Remaining S. & Cen. Americas	1,490
Total S. & Cen. Americas	**5,925**
Austria	120
Belgium	280
Bulgaria	3
Czechoslovakia	7
Denmark	202
Finland	22
France	2,523
German Democratic Republic	4
Germany	1,588
Greece	78
Hungary	6
Iceland	4
Ireland	25
Italy	1,104
Luxembourg	8
Malta	7
Netherlands	370
Norway	64
Poland	3
Portugal	81
Romania	2

Spain	624
Sweden	156
Switzerland	299
United Kingdom	1,227
U.S.S.R.	4
Yugoslavia	21
Total Europe	**8,832**
China	2
China (Taiwan)	1
Cyprus	3
Eastern Mediterranean Region	36
Hong Kong	6
India	9
Indonesia	1
Isreal	43
Japan	59
Jordan	3
Lebanon	3
Malaysia	1
Philippines	10
Qatar	9
Republic of Korea	1
Singapore	2
Sri Lanka	2
Thailand	12
Turkey	21
Total Asia	**224**
Australia	758
French Polynesia	1
New Zealand	54
Tonga	1
Total Oceania	**814**
Algeria	5
Angola	6
Benin	3
Botswana	13

Burundi	569
Burkina Faso	26
Cameroon	25
Cape Verde	4
Central Africa	254
Chad	1
Congo	250
Cote D'Ivoire	250
Ethiopia	19
Gabon	13
Gambia	14
Ghana	145
Guinea	4
Guinea-Bissau	16
Kenya	964
Lesotho	2
Liberia	2
Malawi	13
Mauritius	1
Mozambique	4
Nigeria	5
Reunion	1
Rwanda	705
Senegal	27
South Africa	93
Sudan	12
Swaziland	7
Tanzania	1,608
Tunisia	11
Uganda	2,369
Zaire	335
Zambia	536
Zimbabwe	380
Total Africa	**8,693**
Estimated World Total	**80,912**

Classification of AIDS cases in Canada*

	Alive	Dead	Total	(%)
ADULT cases by risk category				
Homosexual/				
bisexual activity	612	684	1296	(81.6)
Intravenous drug use	2	7	9	(0.6)
Both of the above	16	26	42	(2.6)
Recipient of blood/				
blood products	24	47	71	(4.5)
Heterosexual activity				
a) origin in endemic area	29	56	85	(5.4)
b) sexual contact with				
person at risk	24	17	41	(2.6)
No identified risk factors	16	28	44	(2.8)

CHILDREN (Under 15 years old) by risk category

	Male	Female	Total	(%)
Perinatal transmission	12	17	29	(87.9)
Recipient of blood/				
blood products	2	2	4	(12.1)
Other	0	0	0	(0)

Total Males (adults and children)	1521
Total Females (adults and children)	101
OVERALL TOTAL (adults and children)	1622

*As of March 7, 1988
Source: Federal Centre for AIDS

Classification of AIDS cases in the U.S.*

Adult Cases by Risk Category	Number	(%)
Homosexual/bisexual male	34,687	(70)
Intravenous drug abuser	9,475	(18)
Homosexual male/IV drug abuser	4,016	(7)
Hemophilia/coagulation disorder	552	(1)
Heterosexual cases	2,169	(4)
Transfusion, blood/components	1,297	(2)
Undetermined	1,664	(3)
Adult/Adolescent total	53,858	
Children (under age 13) total	865	
GRAND TOTAL	54,723 **	

*As of March 7, 1988
**Of this figure 30,715 or 56% are deceased
Source: Centers for Disease Control, Atlanta Ga.

AIDS Cases Reported in Canada by Province*

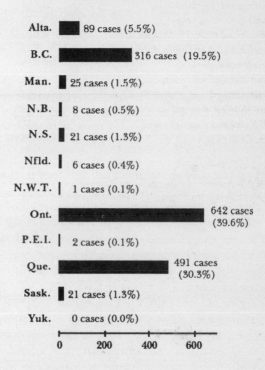

Alta.		89 cases (5.5%)
B.C.		316 cases (19.5%)
Man.		25 cases (1.5%)
N.B.		8 cases (0.5%)
N.S.		21 cases (1.3%)
Nfld.		6 cases (0.4%)
N.W.T.		1 cases (0.1%)
Ont.		642 cases (39.6%)
P.E.I.		2 cases (0.1%)
Que.		491 cases (30.3%)
Sask.		21 cases (1.3%)
Yuk.		0 cases (0.0%)

Total   1622**

*as of March 7, 1988

**of this total, 886 or 54.6% are deceased.

Source: Federal Centre for AIDS

How does HIV spread?

HIV is found primarily in the blood, semen or vaginal fluid of an infected person, and is spread when any one of these enters into another person's body (bloodstream). This can happen through:

a) Sexual contact with an infected person. In Canada, this is the most common means of transmission.

b) Sharing contaminated needles or syringes for the abuse of intravenous drugs.

c) An infected mother who transmits the virus to her baby before or at birth, or through breast-feeding.

d) The transfusion or injection of infected blood or blood products. This means of contracting the virus is very rare because, since November 1985, the Canadian Red Cross, which handles all blood donations in Canada, tests every unit of blood collected for HIV as well as taking other increased precautions. The tests are extremely sensitive, and any contaminated blood is discarded.

e) Accidents with infected blood in hospitals and laboratories. This has happened most often with needlestick injuries to health care workers handling syringes containing infected blood. Even though several thousand health care workers exposed to the virus have been studied, only 12 have been known to be infected worldwide. There is a very low risk of infection by this means.

There is no evidence that AIDS can be transmitted through air, water, food or casual body contact. Although the virus has been found in very small traces in tears and saliva, there have been no cases to date of anyone becoming infected from contact with these body fluids. The amount of virus present may be too small to cause an infection.

Not everyone infected with HIV has AIDS or may develop AIDS. Some people, having been exposed to the virus, carry it in their bloodstreams and exhibit no symptoms. This is perhaps the most concerning characteristic of the virus, since other people can then acquire the infection if they engage in risk behaviors with the infected person.

While some people may develop mild symptoms, others may have more persistent symptoms. This stage of the course of the infection is called symptomatic HIV infection. Symptoms include persistent swelling of the lymph glands, night sweats, diarrhea, fever, fatigue or weight loss. These symptoms may occur as the HIV infection worsens and more damage to the immune system results. In combination, these symptoms are termed AIDS-Related Complex (ARC).

The most advanced and fatal stage of HIV infection is defined as AIDS when immune system damage is so severe that other life-threatening infections, cancers or brain disease occurs.

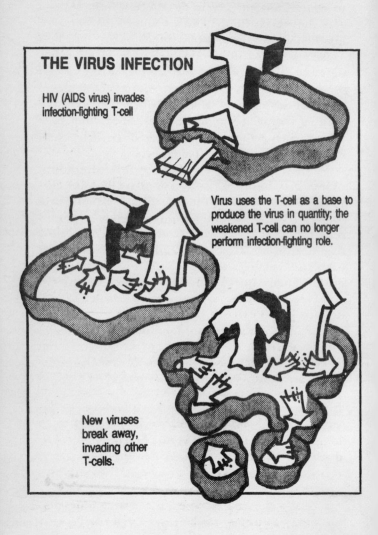

THE VIRUS INFECTION

HIV (AIDS virus) invades infection-fighting T-cell

Virus uses the T-cell as a base to produce the virus in quantity; the weakened T-cell can no longer perform infection-fighting role.

New viruses break away, invading other T-cells.

What happens when someone is exposed to HIV?
If the virus is able to enter the body in sufficient numbers and finds its way into the bloodstream, it can have devastating effects. The virus in the bloodstream will seek out a particular form of white blood cell that is essential to the effectiveness of the immune system. This particular cell is called a "T-helper lymphocyte" and one of its functions is to "orchestrate" the immune system in the event of the attack from infection.

The virus attaches to the surface of the lymphocyte and then penetrates its body. The virus constructs an enzyme, (called reverse-transcriptase), that "reprograms" the genetic DNA of the lymphocyte. The lymphocyte ceases to be an effective part of the immune system and instead becomes a factory for producing HIV. The virus reproduces inside the lymphocyte, ultimately killing it in the process. The newly constructed viruses then exit from the lymphocyte in which they have reproduced and seek other lymphocytes in which to continue the reproductive process.

As the virus continues its reproduction, the body loses increasing numbers of lymphocytes, thereby slowly diminishing the ability of the immune system to function properly and fight off infectious diseases. The T-helper lymphocyte is intended to be long-lived, and the body is not designed to reproduce the large quantities of new lymphocytes to replace those lost to HIV. Ordinarily, these lymphocytes would live 25 years. So, the "incubation period" for AIDS – the time between infection and development of symptoms – can be several years as the virus slowly destroys the lymphocytes, promoting a gradual deterioration of the immune system.

It has been learned recently that HIV not only attacks the immune system but also penetrates the brain destroying cells and thus directly causing loss of brain function.

What are the symptoms of HIV infection?

Some symptoms of HIV infection are not specific, and it is important to understand that the following list resembles the symptoms of other diseases. Many of them may be purely symptoms of stress:

☐ Unexplained, persistent fatigue
☐ Unexplained fever, shaking chills, or drenching night sweats lasting longer than several weeks
☐ Unexplained weight loss greater than ten pounds that cannot be attributed to dieting
☐ Swollen glands (enlarged lymph nodes usually in the neck, armpits or groin) which are otherwise unexplained and last more than two months
☐ Persistent diarrhea
☐ Unexplained bleeding from any body opening or from growths on the skin or mucous membranes

Other symptoms may indicate specific conditions associated with AIDS:

☐ Pink to purple flat or raised blotches or bumps occurring on or under the skin, inside the mouth, nose, eyelids or rectum. Initially, they may resemble bruises but do not disappear. They are usually harder than the skin around them.

☐ Persistent white spots or unusual blemishes in the mouth. This is known as 'thrush' – a thick, whitish coating on the tongue or in the throat which may be accompanied by a sore throat.

☐ Persistent dry cough (that cannot be attributed to smoking) which has lasted too long to be caused by a common respiratory infection, especially if accompanied by shortness of breath.

☐ Headache, weakness or numbness in arms or legs, poor concentration, confusion.

A doctor will try to make a diagnosis based on these symptoms, a past history of risk behaviors and supporting physical and laboratory tests, including a test for the presence in the blood of antibodies to HIV.

What are some of the diseases affecting persons with AIDS?

In persons with AIDS (PWAs), specific diseases have taken advantage of the opportunity presented by the damaged immune system. About 80% of the AIDS cases reported have had one or both of two rather rare diseases.

The first is called Pneumocystis carinii pneumonia (PCP) which is a parasitic infection of the lungs and has symptoms similar to other forms of pneumonia. This pneumonia is found in over 50% of AIDS patients in Canada. Shortness of breath, coughing, fever and a pattern of risk behaviors, are often the symptoms that first lead a doctor to suspect AIDS in a patient.

The second disease is called Kaposi's sarcoma (KS) which is a rare type of cancer of the blood vessels and lymphatic system, and may occur anywhere on the surface of the skin or internally on other tissue surfaces (e.g. inside the mouth). KS may first appear as a blue-violet or brownish spot on the skin. The spot or spots persist, and may grow larger. As it progresses, it can spread to other tissues, such as the lymph nodes, digestive tract and lungs.

Other opportunistic infections include tuberculosis, cytomegalo-virus, herpes virus, and parasites such as toxoplasmosis or cryptosporidia.

Cases of tuberculosis (TB) for example, have increased in the United States since 1986 primarily among AIDS patients that contracted the disease through intravenous drug abuse. TB is generally perceived as a lung infection however in 75% of AIDS patients with TB the disease has been found outside the lungs in bone, brain and other organs and can be an early indication that a person's immune system is failing. Although TB if untreated, is transmissible by air there is no possibility of contracting AIDS from an AIDS patient infected with TB.

It has also been found that the brain and other parts of the nervous system are infected and damaged directly by HIV and many patients, perhaps a majority, will develop some impairment. This may first appear as forgetfulness and poor concentration, but later progress in some to confusion, disorientation and dementia.

Who is most at risk of contracting AIDS?

In theory, anyone can get AIDS – it depends on your behavior. Any sexually active person who is not maintaining a mutually monogamous relationship (both partners faithful) and does not take precautionary measures to exercise safer sex practices is at risk of contracting AIDS.

Homosexual and bisexual men who engage in the practice of anal intercourse without precautions are at very great risk and represent the highest percentage of AIDS cases. In Canada, this group represents over 82% of all reported cases, while in the United States, it represents 66% of reported cases.

Intravenous drug abusers who share contaminated needles or syringes are the second group to be most concerned and represent 17% of the AIDS cases in the United States. This group, however, only represents 0.6% of the AIDS cases in Canada.

The low rate of cases from IV drug abuse in Canada is a similar pattern to other countries such as Australia. The difference from American figures may be due to a smaller drug abuse problem, but more importantly it may stem from the fact that needles and syringes are more readily available here, and are therefore not shared as frequently. They can be purchased at many pharmacies over the counter, while in the U.S. a doctor's prescription is usually required. Nevertheless, drug abuse by itself is dangerous in any situation, particularly if equipment is shared.

Other risk situations include:

☐ Those who have heterosexual relationships with people who may be in the high risk groups.

☐ Persons who received blood transfusions of infected blood or blood products prior to the initiation of Red Cross screening of all blood donations in November 1985.

☐ Children who contract HIV from their infected mother, before or at birth.

Who should be examined for AIDS?

Doctors are asked to examine and counsel a number of different groups of people who are concerned that they may have AIDS. Laboratory testing for evidence of HIV infection may be suggested in the following situations:

☐ Someone who is showing symptoms of AIDS or an AIDS-related illness (swollen lymph glands, persistent night sweats, diarrhea, rapid loss of weight). It should be noted, however, that any number of other conditions also cause these symptoms).

☐ A health care worker who has had accidental and significant exposure to body fluids (e.g. blood) of an AIDS patient.

☐ A person with a history of high risk behaviors, such as;

* homosexual and bisexual men who have not practised safer sex
* heterosexual men and women who have had many different sexual partners
* people who received many blood or blood product transfusions since 1980 (when AIDS probably first occurred in Canada) and before November 1985 (when the Red Cross began screening blood donations)
* sexual partners of those with high risk behaviors, or a positive test for antibodies to HIV
* prostitutes (male and female)

If you have not engaged in a high risk behavior and are not showing any symptoms of AIDS-related illnesses, it does not mean that you are safe from the virus. You should continue to engage in safer sex practices.

Anyone who may be considering being tested for HIV antibodies should seek pre and post-test counselling from their doctors. Local health authorities and/or local AIDS groups may also be consulted.

Remember: To undertake testing without pre and post-test counselling can have serious psychological ramifications. You may test negative and still be harboring the virus. Pre and post-test counselling is of paramount importance.

Is it easy to get AIDS?

No. HIV infection is not easily transmissible. It is transmitted only by specific risk behaviours. It is not nearly as contagious, for example, as the flu, colds, measles, and other more common diseases. These common viruses can be spread through the air by coughs, sneezes, etc. HIV cannot be spread in this manner.

The virus is not transmissible through eating or drinking from common utensils. You cannot catch the virus from toilet seats, swimming pools (saunas, whirlpools), water fountains, hugging, a handshake, or from using common facilities such as telephones or laundry and locker rooms. Extensive studies of families of Persons with AIDS (PWAs) have found not one case of the virus being spread through everyday contact. No one has ever caught HIV infection from kissing, and althought the virus has been isolated from saliva, the concentrations are thought to be too low to cause infection in others.

How can I reduce the risk of getting AIDS?

The following is a list of precautions that can be taken by the general public and by persons in special risk groups to eliminate or reduce the risk of contracting or spreading AIDS:

☐ Abstinence from sex, or maintaining a mutually monogamous relationship with a partner who has not been exposed to HIV are the surest ways to eliminate risk.

☐ Avoiding sexual contact with any person whose past history and current health status is not known.

☐ Exercising safer sex practices at all times.

☐ Avoiding abuse of intravenous (IV) drugs.

☐ Not sharing needles or syringes (boiling does not guarantee sterility).

☐ Avoiding sexual contact with persons who abuse IV drugs.

☐ Proper use of a latex condom during sexual intercourse will decrease the risk of AIDS.

☐ Not sharing toothbrushes, razors or other personal implements that could become contaminated with blood.

☐ Health workers, laboratory personnel, funeral directors and others whose work may involve contact with body fluid should strictly follow recommended safety procedures to minimize exposure to AIDS, hepatitis B and other bloodborne diseases.

☐ Persons who are at increased risk of AIDS or who have positive HIV anti-body test results should not donate blood, plasma, body organs, sperm or other tissue.

☐ Persons with positive AIDS antibody test results should have regular medical checkups, and take special precautions against exchanging bodily fluids during sexual activity.

☐ Women who have positive HIV antibody test results should recognize that if they become pregnant their children are at increased risk of contracting AIDS.

Is there a cure for AIDS?

No. Currently there are no drugs available anywhere that have been approved or that have been shown to cure AIDS, although the search for an effective treatment is being pursued vigorously. Best estimates suggest that a cure or a vaccine for AIDS will be several years forthcoming.

Some drugs have been discovered that inhibit the action of HIV such as a drug known as AZT. This is Azidothyoidine, a prescription drug that was originally derived from the sperm of herring but is now synthetically produced. It has been approved for use in the United States and is currently being provided in Canada, free of charge to patients, for trial purposes that began across Canada in November, 1986.

When the drug therapy was first introduced in Canada by its manufacturer Burroughs Wellcome, only AIDS patients with pneumonocystis carinii pneumonia (PCP) were eligible to receive AZT which is marketed under the brand name Retrovir. An agreement (May '87) between the manufacturer and the Department of National Health and Welfare and the Provinces now permits the drug to be administered to AIDS patients with other opportunistic infections involving viral, parasitic and bacterial diseases, and to individuals with severe symptomatic AIDS virus infection and a low T-4 cell count. Uniform criteria for enrolling patients now apply across Canada.

Availability of AZT continues to be the responsibility of approved clinical investigators who administer the drug under strict medical conditions. The investigators continue to participate in monitoring and data-collection on drug efficacy and patient safety.

AZT is made available internationally by the manufacturer on a "share" basis according to World Health Organization statistics on AIDS cases worldwide. Canada receives a full share of that supply.

In January, 1987 a California drug company announced that a drug already approved for treatment of children's infections could also prevent some people exposed to HIV from developing the disease. The anti-viral agent, **Ribavirin**, also known as **Virazone**, has shown itself effective in clinical trials on patients with Lymphadenopathy Syndrome (a disease known as LAS that often precedes the development of AIDS). However, this drug is still being tested and evaluated.

Laboratory tests in Britain using the drug **Fusidin** (Acid) commonly used for treating wound infections prevented HIV from penetrating healthy cells. Similar tests in Denmark on one AIDS patient resulted in weight gain and no side effects. This drug is inexpensive, non-toxic and easily available and is currently undergoing extensive testing in Denmark and British hospitals.

An anti-AIDS vaccine is now being tested on a group of volunteers in the U.S. and Canada by a bio-pharmaceutical company called MicroGeneSys Inc. and a team of Canadian researchers. The company is the first to be awarded approval from the U.S. Food and Drug Administration to conduct human trials, the results of which will not be completed until the mid-1990s. The vaccine uses a purified protein produced by insects that mimics the surface protein on the AIDS virus and has produced very positive antibody responses against the virus in laboratory animals. All volunteers currently being tested are HIV-free and have agreed to exercise 'safer sex' practices while undergoing the study.

Beware of health frauds concerning AIDS. There are no anti-AIDS formulas, disease fighting douches to protect against AIDS, or health foods that can prevent AIDS or protect against the AIDS virus. Despite what you might hear or read in catalogue or magazine advertisements, there is no cure or AIDS preventive product. Any breakthrough concerning a treatment or cure for AIDS will be announced by Health and Welfare Canada.

Should I donate blood? Are blood transfusions safe?
By all means feel free to donate blood. There is NO possibility of contracting HIV from the needle used when you donate blood. A new needle is used for each donor. If, however, you feel there is any

remote possibility that you could be an HIV carrier, you SHOULD NOT donate blood.

Since November 1, 1985, the Red Cross has been screening all blood donations for HIV antibodies. Blood that tests positive for the antibody is not used for transfusions.

Do not donate blood for the purpose of determining whether or not you are an HIV carrier. This will put others at risk. Consult your physician regarding testing. If the Red Cross finds these antibodies in your blood, your results will be reported automatically to the local health authorities.

Why is AIDS considered a homosexual disease?

While medical researchers and physicians are loathe to tie the disease to any one sociological group, no discussion about the spread of AIDS can ignore that part of our society which has been struck the hardest by the epidemic.

Initially described as 'The Gay Plague', AIDS was already epidemic in the homosexual community long before it came under the international spotlight. For many in this community, a lifestyle involving multiple sexual partners and anal intercourse provided the disease with an environment in which to spread effectively.

While many tried to divert public attention away from the most-visible victims of the disease, the media rarely reported an AIDS news story without referring to it as 'the gay' or 'homosexual' disease. This has left an indelible impression in the minds of many people that only recently seems to be diminishing as AIDS becomes more visible in the heterosexual community.

You, a fluent French speaker,

WHY NOT?

"I can teach you a newer, better, *faster* way. But don't just take my word for it. Send for this FREE Sample Lesson Cassette and see for yourself."

Joanne Carper
President

CONTEMPORARY FRENCH
Free Sample Lessons

Although the gay community may have suffered the initial onslaught of AIDS, it has clearly been established that the virus is completely undiscriminating concerning those it attacks. Recent figures suggest that up to 27% (Western hemisphere) of people currently afflicted with HIV are in fact heterosexuals (this figure includes children and intravenous drug users) and this percentage is steadily on the increase.

In Africa, AIDS strikes men and women in almost equal numbers and heterosexual spread is most common. It is clear then that AIDS should not be considered exclusive to any one group; rather, it is associated with certain behavior patterns.

Is there any possibility of contracting the Human Immunodeficiency Virus from animals?
No. There is no evidence to support an even remote possibility of HIV being contracted from animals including household pets.

Publicity that appeared in February 1987 concerning an AIDS-like virus found in U.S. cats was based on the findings of scientists at the University of California at Davis. The virus called feline T-lymphotropic lentivirus (FTLV) is genetically distinct from the virus that produces AIDS in humans, but it causes similar symptoms; swollen lymph nodes, weight loss, diarrhea, respiratory infections, anemia and parasitic infections. The disease may pose a serious threat to feline health, but may also make cats useful in AIDS research. FTLV poses no threat to human health.

Can insects such as mosquitos carry HIV?

No. Insects such as mosquitos do not transmit AIDS. Mosquitos only spread diseases that use the insect as part of the disease's life-cycle. Malaria, for instance, is a parasitic infestation. The parasite has to spend part of its life in an anopheles mosquito in order to mature, before the mosquito can spread the disease.

However, bloodborne diseases such as syphilis, hepatitis and AIDS are not spread by biting insects.

Also, mosquitos don't go immediately from person to person. A mosquito will usually bite and feed about once every 48 hours. Even if the virus were there, it would be in minute quantities and would die before the next bite.

If mosquitos were transmitting AIDS, we would see many more cases of AIDS in those parts of the world where mosquitos are most common, and in all age/sex categories in their countries, not just young adults.

How is my life insurance affected by AIDS?

Most life and health insurance contracts are issued on a non-cancellable basis – once the contract is issued it cannot be modified or withdrawn by the insurer, except in cases where information was withheld at the time of the contract application.

As long as the necessary premiums are paid, the contract continues to be in effect and all claims will be paid. If, however, you are applying for life or health insurance and happen to:

a) have been exposed to HIV see page 38 – **Who is most at risk of contracting AIDS?**)

b) have tested positive in an HIV antibody test

c) be suffering (although perhaps not visibly) from
   any AIDS-related illness (ARC) or related symptoms
...your request for insurance will likely not be
granted. If you fail to divulge your current state of
health or status and you are granted insurance, any
likelihood of you or your heirs appreciating the benefits of that insurance is unlikely since you did not
make full disclosure at the time of your application
and your claim will be denied.

Insurance companies may require you to take a
medical examination at the time of your application
and this physical examination usually requires a
blood test. While this test was originally performed
to determine blood factors such as your cholesterol
count, it now may explore the possibility of AIDS
antibodies in your system. Certain groups have suggested that this is a discriminatory practice by the
insurance companies, since the fact that you may
have HIV antibodies in your bloodstream does not
suggest that you will develop AIDS or AIDS-related
illnesses. While it is true that you may not develop
AIDS or AIDS-related illnesses, it should be under-
stood that insurance companies deal with risks, not
with certainties. Everyone who has been exposed to
the virus has a significant extra risk, just as anyone
who has had a recent heart attack has some
increased mortality risk. Insurers evaluate and deal
with these risks; they don't wait until the eventual
outcome is certain.

Efforts are currently underway by the insurance
companies to determine whether it will be possible
to provide at least partial insurance for those who
are unable to obtain full coverage as a result of

AIDS-related risks; for instance, to provide life insurance for deaths which arise from any condition not caused or influenced by AIDS. These efforts are complicated seriously, often by the lack of accurate and complete information on the cause of death, and also by incomplete medical information at this stage on the full impact of HIV on various body systems. However, this possibility is still being explored.

All medical research concerning AIDS is being closely monitored by the insurance industry. However, until a cure or vaccine is on the horizon, insurance companies will continue to adapt risk evaluation and classification procedures. AIDS will definitely have a significant impact in terms of additional benefit payments, and additional insurance costs to all of us. However, existing legislation and safeguards are adequate to ensure the voluntary risk-sharing process of the system is preserved, providing that the spread of AIDS can be controlled through public education and research.

Why are hemophiliacs considered a high risk group?
Hemophiliacs (bleeders) are not considered a high risk group in Canada, although they are often listed with other groups when AIDS statistics are recorded. In most cases those hemophiliacs that have contracted HIV have done so through infusions of blood or blood products prior to the initiation of Red Cross screening of all blood donations (November 1985).

Hemophilia is an inherited disorder in which a specific blood-clotting agent (protein) is lacking in the blood. Hemophiliacs are treated by replacing the missing factor through infusions taken from blood pooled from donors.

There are approximately 3,000 hemophiliacs in Canada and 25,000 in the United States.

I've heard of social clubs that guarantee members are AIDS free. Do they exist in Canada?
Yes, there are such clubs but one should be cautious concerning any guarantees these clubs offer particularly concerning AIDS free membership. Recent studies have indicated that the AIDS virus can remain dormant in the system for anywhere up to fourteen months before the blood develops antibodies to the virus. Even with the regular blood testing these social clubs offer there is no guarantee that a member is not an HIV carrier. Exercising safer sex practices is the best possible way to avoiding contracting AIDS (other than abstaining from sex altogether).

Is there any way I can store my own blood in the event I need it for future surgery?
Private blood banks have started up in Canada and the United States that do provide this service however they are generally considered to be capitalizing on the public's fear of AIDS. Storing ones own blood is unnecessary and expensive at a cost of approximately $235.00 per unit, plus an annual storage fee of about $45.00. It is estimated that any chance of contracting HIV from the carefully-tested blood supplies of the Red Cross is less than one in a million. However, if you have impending surgery (and wish to use your own blood), first speak to yor

doctor about this possibility. The service, called "autologous blood donation," may be available free of charge at major hospitals. Several pints of blood that you donate can be stored for thirty days for use in surgery that can be scheduled in advance.

If AIDS is not highly contagious, why do police and other emergency personnel take the precautions they do, such as using surgical masks and rubber gloves?
Despite the precautions you might see in the media taken by police and other emergency personel, AIDS is not easily transmissable. It is not nearly as contagious, for example, as the flu, colds, measles or other more common diseases. The virus which causes AIDS is found in the blood, semen, or vaginal fluid of an infected person, and is spread when any of these substances enters another person's body (bloodstream). It is true that the AIDS virus has also been isolated in the laboratory from tears and saliva of some infected individuals, but there is not one known case of anyone contracting the disease from tears or saliva.

Police and other emergency personnel are often exposed to blood situations through accidents, the need for forcible restraint, threats, etc. Although the risk is slight, small nicks or cuts on the hands could conceivably become the means for the AIDS virus to gain access to a healthy individual if they were to become blood-soaked. It has happened, for example, for inmates in prison to try and intimidate guards by biting their own lips enabling them to spit blood at prison personnel while declaring they are AIDS virus carriers.

Although surgical masks are considered by many to be an extreme and unnecessary caution, waterproof gloves have become standard issue for many police and other emergency personnel nationally.

I'm Catholic. How can I practise safe sex?

Father James M. Wingle, Vice-Rector, St. Augustine's Seminary in Toronto, was kind enough to respond to this question on behalf of the writer. While Father Wingle is a reputable and well qualified moral theologian, with all due respect, the following opinions that he expresses do not necessarily reflect those of the publishers, editors, and/or the writer. His text has been reproduced in its entirety.

Sexuality, from the perspective of Catholic teaching, is a wonderful gift of God who created human life. It is an integral and profound dimension of the life of every human person. This beautiful feature of human existence, sexuality, needs to be held in respectful esteem as the gift it is from the Giver of life itself, that is from God.

In the first book of the Bible, God looks upon the sexual beings He has made, man and woman fashioned in His own image, and we read there: "God saw all that He had made, and it was very good" (Genesis 1:31). What the church claims about this gift, based on the Scriptures (the Bible) and her long years of experience as teacher, is that God had something in mind in creating man and woman differently. This means simply that there is a God-given meaning and purpose in human sexuality. Expressions of sexuality, which are a kind of language, ought to be loving, joyful, healthy, responsible and life-giving. They are so when they are well integrated into the totality of a person's life and when they are respectful of their God-given meaning.

Genital sexual union, which is one part of the whole sexual language of the body, is intended to be a profound expression of mutual love and full mutual giving and receiving which is proper to the partners of a permanent and faithful union. What sexual union says is that "we two distinct and different people are one flesh." The joining of two bodies in sexual intercourse speaks of a union of the lives of the two partners in love and a radical openness to the new life which may flow from this action. Outside of such an exclusive covenant-type of relationship, which we know as marriage, the expression of genital activity fails to achieve its true meaning. The Irish Bishops speak this truth with particular power and beauty in their Pastoral Letter when they write:

"By sexual union, a man and a woman say to each other: I love you. There is nobody else in all the world I love in the way I love you. I love you just for being you. I want you to become even more wonderful than you are. I want to share my life and my world with you. I want you to share your life and your world with me. I want us to build a new life together, which will be our future. I need you. I can't live without you. I need you to love me, and to love me not just now but always. I will be faithful to you not just now but always. I will never let you down or walk out on you. I will never put anyone else in place of you. I will stay with you through thick and thin. I will be responsible for you and I want you to be responsible for me, for us, no matter what happens."

Genital activity belongs within the context of the kind of relationship described above by the Catholic Bishops of Ireland. Surrounded by an exclusive love commitment of the partners, protected by the promise of lasting faithfulness, such sexual union can achieve the good ends for which it was intended by God, namely, the union of the spouses and the begetting of new life. The use of genital expression in any other context is incapable of achieving these good ends, and thus we can describe it as morally disordered. When people engage their sexual capacity in extra-marital relationships they are in effect saying two contradictory things. No matter what the personal intention of the sexual partners may be, this inner meaning of the sexual union is denied in whole or in part if either of the partners take action to frustrate the principle consequences of their sexual union.

The sad influence of sin plays its part in the sexual experience of people today as it has throughout the history of the human family. We are inclined towards selfishness in the sexual, as in other spheres of life. Much of the social value in present day popular culture seems to see sexual activity as chiefly a self-indulgent play thing, or worse still – as a consumer commodity to be bought and sold. Sexual morality as held and taught by the Catholic tradition aims to protect people from the loss of dignity and nobility which results from disordered sexual practices. Education in the true meaning of love towards self and others, which is the aim of morality, must separate what is authentic love in sexual behavior from what pretends to be love.

In addition to the primary moral disorder of using genital sexual expression outside of its proper place in marriage, there is the secondary but serious threat to physical health and well-being from sexually transmitted diseases. Among such diseases the appearance and alarming spread of the AIDS virus has added a whole new and lethal dimension to the matter. Since the virus is transmitted through bodily fluids, a person who engages in casual sexual activity may literally be risking his or her life. To expose oneself or others to such a risk is profoundly wrong. While fear of disease is far from the main reason for promoting a chaste life, it is nevertheless a powerful practical incentive.

Not a few voices promote the notion that the use of condoms is a good idea as a protection against infection from the AIDS virus. Others seem to want to launch campaigns in the schools and in the media to promote the use of condoms as a means towards so-called "safe sex". In the first place, from what has been said above, it is clear that promotion of casual and irresponsible sexual behavior by the suggestion that using condoms can make such activity safe is morally offensive and simply untrue. What we ought to convey is a truly healthy notion of sexuality and the need for responsible control of self in response to the powerful urgency of sexual appetite. In addition to the serious falsification of the meaning of sexual intercourse by removing its capacity to engender life, which condoms do, the protection from the disease of AIDS which it affords is at best dubious. In practical terms, it is far from unknown that condoms break during use and even when they do not, it is not unusual that in the hands of young people and not-so-young people who are deeply aroused and excited sexually, they are improperly used.

How should we view the choice which someone makes to engage in sexual activity with a person other than his or her marriage partner and uses a condom to try to reduce the risk of infection from the AIDS virus? It is somewhat life a thief asking "How can I reduce the harm caused by my action of stealing?" The primary action of sexual union outside of marriage remains seriously disordered and morally wrong for the reasons detailed above. The use of a device such as a condom to attempt to prevent the transmission or acquisition of AIDS, if the person is going to go ahead with the wrongful sexual action in any case, might help to prevent to some degree a still further evil, that is the spread of the disease. The moral evaluation of such a choice would be somewhat similar to weighing the difference of a burglar's use of refined instruments to break into someone's house as compared to his using a sledgehammer and dynamite; in either case the serious wrong of burglary remains, though in the first case – a lesser evil results.

In summary then, a Catholic faith perspective on so-called "safe sex" would define safe sex quite differently than is generally the case in society at large. Genital sexual expression ought to be reserved to one's permanent marriage partner as a expression of love and exclusive faithfulness. In this context it is both "safe" and good.

AIDS TESTING

What are the tests for AIDS?
There are three types of tests that may help in diagnosing AIDS or AIDS-related conditions:

☐ A blood screening test for the HIV antibody
☐ A test of the immune system
☐ A test which identifies HIV itself

The blood screening test for the HIV antibody is the most popular currently being used. When any virus gets into a person's blood, the body reacts by producing specific antibodies. For HIV, these antibodies do not destroy the virus, but serve as an indication of its presence in the bloodstream. An antibody test is not called "positive" until the test is repeated and the initial results confirmed.

If HIV antibodies are found in a person's blood, it doesn't necessarily mean that the person has AIDS or will go on to develop AIDS. Nor does it mean the person is immune to AIDS. (Usually antibodies protect a person from a disease, but this is not the case with HIV antibodies).

If antibodies are found, it means that the person has been exposed and infected some time in the past and is now potentially infectious to others. Although it is a very debatable issue at the moment, it is variously estimated that between 10% and 50% of those people who have the antibodies will actually develop AIDS. Some people have the virus in their bloodstream for a number of years and never develop symptoms of AIDS. Others develop AIDS after the virus has been present in the blood for a few months.

The HIV antibody test has been found to be the most reliable indicator of exposure and infectiousness, and is the most widely used.

People with AIDS have many severe problems with their immune systems. A doctor can order *immune system tests*, special studies of the white blood cells and antibodies of the immune system in people with suspicious symptoms – if the doctor thinks these tests are necessary.

Identification of HIV itself is a very specialized procedure used in research which cultures and isolates the actual virus from a person's blood. This procedure is not widely used for diagnosing HIV infection because of high cost and duration of the procedure. Researchers are currently working to develop simpler ways to test for the presence of the virus in the blood.

CONCERNING THE BLOOD SCREENING TEST FOR THE AIDS VIRUS ANTIBODY:

What does a positive test mean?
If you test positive, it means that antibodies to HIV have been found in your blood. A positive test result tells you that you have been exposed to the virus at some point and have reacted.

☐ It DOES NOT mean that you have AIDS or an AIDS-related illness

☐ It DOES NOT mean you will be ill in the future

☐ It DOES NOT mean that you are immune to AIDS

☐ It DOES, however, mean that as you have been exposed to the virus, you are considered to be a *carrier* of the virus. It also means that you may have up to a 50% chance of developing AIDS in the next five to ten years. All confirmed antibody positive individuals must be considered infectious and capable of passing the virus to others. Recent studies have confirmed this probability.

What does a negative test mean?
Testing negative means that no antibodies to HIV have been found in your blood. However, this DOES NOT mean that you haven't been infected by the virus. You may have been infected recently enough that your body hasn't yet had time to produce antibodies. Recent studies have indicated that the AIDS virus can remain dormant in the system for anywhere up to one year before the blood develops anti-bodies to the virus but it is known that most people develop antibodies within three weeks to three months. Also, negative test results DO NOT tell you whether you are capable of passing on the virus (if it is there) to another person.

It is very important, even with a negative test result, to still avoid risk behaviors.

If there is so much the test can't tell us, what is it good for?
The HIV antibody test is used primarily not to screen people, but to screen their blood, tissue, organs or sperm, to assess their health, to assist in diagnosis and to protect others from being exposed.

In addition:
☐ The Canadian Red Cross uses the test to screen blood donations. Even though the test cannot tell

us if the virus itself is present, it gives us evidence of potentially infectious blood, and in those instances the blood is discarded.

☐ The test can be used to reduce the risk of infection in organ transplants.

☐ Sperm banks can use the test to tell whether donors of semen are free of infection.

The test can also help people who run only a small risk of having been exposed to the virus at some time in the past. For instance, anyone who has had a blood transfusion since 1979 has a very slight chance (about one in 500,000) of exposure.

People who test positive should know what precautions to take. This is why any testing must be only a part of an appropriate counselling process.

Who gets to see my test results?

In most provinces, if you get a positive test result through your doctor's office, a clinic, or after donated blood has been screened by the Red Cross, your results will be reported to local or provincial public health authorities. In future, they may contact you to offer counselling. They may also offer counselling to any sexual partners you may have had, and to recommend they be tested as well.

These results are confidential, and your doctor will not provide this information to employers, insurance companies, or anyone else, unless your consent is given.

Before taking the test in other situations, you should consider that:

☐ A positive result could also be interpreted by people to mean that you are a homosexual or a drug user. Others might wrongly assume that a person with a positive result is infectious in casual social situations.

☐ Results could be required in court cases, such as those involving child custody.

☐ Most insurance companies deny coverage to individuals who have tested positive.

☐ Employers might demand that people take the test before being employed or promoted, as the U.S. military is now doing.

In Canada, not much legislation exists to limit uses of the test. However, the test remains voluntary.

If you are concerned about who may see your test result, you should discuss the issue with your doctor. In some areas, you can have the HIV antibody test done anonymously, with results are linked only to a code number and not to your name. For information on anonymous testing, if available in your area, you should contact your local community AIDS group, which is listed in the back of this book.

At this time, such testing is not readily available in much of Canada.

It is important to mention that public health agencies which follow up with the doctor for a given individual with a positive test, do so to ensure that the individual is receiving proper interpretation and health education about the meaning of the test. Confidentiality is strictly observed.

The thought that I might test positive to the HIV antibody test frightens me. What should I do?
Whether to be tested or not is a decision that only you can make. However, if you think there is any possibility that you might test positive for the HIV

antibody test (see page 40 – **Who should be examined for AIDS**), you should discuss the test with your doctor. He/she will advise you, and inform you if you live in a province requiring that he/she report your test results to local or provincial authorities, and will answer your concerns.

Pre-test and post-test counselling is highly recommended, first with your doctor, and possibly with your local AIDS community support group.

Remember: Testing positive to the HIV antibody test does not mean that AIDS will develop, but the test result may help you make some serious decisions concerning your future lifestyle.

Is there an HIV antibody test I can take at home?
No, not at this time and the likelihood of such a test being made available in Canada is very remote. At a Toronto press conference, held December 11, 1986, an American company called Pilot Laboratories, a division of Redington Incorp., Stanford, Conn., introduced a kit that would provide an HIV antibody screening test for both home and doctors' use. Any product of this nature would have to be approved by the federal government before being sold in Canada to ensure adequate quality control..

If a person has AIDS, a related illness or a positive HIV antibody test, what should he or she do?
A doctor will examine the person, request additional testing and monitor the patient as necessary. The doctor will also counsel the person or arrange for counselling as required.

Since the blood and bodily fluids of someone with a positive antibody test are infectious, the following precautions are recommended:

☐ Tell any sexual partners.

☐ Have safer sex – have sexual contact without penetration. Don't indulge in any activities in which semen or blood enters the vagina, anus or mouth. Or abstain from sex.

☐ If you must have sex, use a latex condom and use it properly – follow the instructions on the package very carefully. (See page 75 – **How to use a condom properly**).

☐ If you want to be especially careful, abstain from "deep-kissing". The risk is very slight, but HIV has been found in small quantities in the saliva of infected people and might get into another person's bloodstream through cuts or sores in the mouth.

☐ Don't have acupuncture, ear piercing, tattoos or electrolysis treatments.

☐ Consult your doctor before planning a pregnancy. Infants born to infected women may acquire the virus in the womb and those who do usually die in infancy. The virus has also been found in breast milk. If you have an infant, check with your doctor before breast-feeding.

☐ Don't abuse drugs. If you do, never share needles or syringes.

☐ Don't donate blood, plasma, body organs, sperm or other tissue.

☐ Don't share personal items such as toothbrushes, razors or other implements that could become contaminated with blood.

☐ Inform anyone who provides you with health care

and may have contact with your blood or other bodily fluids – such as doctors, dentists, or nurses – so they can take adequate precautions.
- ☐ Have regular medical check-ups.
- ☐ Take care of your general health – eat properly, get plenty of rest and exercise regularly.

How can I help someone I know with AIDS?

The same way you would help anyone you know who has a fatal disease. While you may experience a feeling of helplessness, your frustration will not be as great as that of the person with AIDS (PWA). Fear of the unknown and isolation seem to be the biggest factors affecting the AIDS patient.

Your demonstration of support, compassion and understanding will never be more appreciated.

The above question was posed to a PWA in Vancouver. Here is his response:

"It is important that people understand that the person with AIDS does not want to be treated as a social outcast or thought of as a 'victim' or 'leper'. It is vitally important to our mental health and physical being that we be allowed to maintain hope, think positively and 'get on' with our lives.

"It is inappropriate for people to be constantly asking 'How are you feeling?' or 'Has there been any new developments?' It is particularly hurtful when meeting someone for the first time and they turn away or cover their mouth when they discover I have AIDS. What they are forgetting is that it is my immune system that is destroyed. There is more likelihood of me catching something from them than the reverse."

Am I at risk helping a friend with AIDS?

No, you are not. Unless you are indulging in unprotected sexual activity or other risk behaviors with your friend, there is virtually no chance of your contracting HIV If you are nursing a friend with AIDS and are handling bodily fluids, follow the guidelines outlined in this book under the sub-heading **AIDS and the Health Care Worker** (see page 115).

Why is HIV testing not mandatory?

The most popular HIV test is the one designed to identify antibodies to the virus in the blood. When any virus gets into a person's bloodstream, the body's immune system reacts by immediately producing specific antibodies to fight off that infection. In the case of HIV however, these antibodies cannot destroy the virus, but only serve as an indication of its presence in the blood. Because HIV can remain dormant in the system for up to 14 months before becoming active and consequently stimulating the immune system into generating antibodies, anyone tested during that fourteen month period could test negative to the virus. They would however still be a carrier of the disease and be capable of transmitting it. While mandatory HIV testing might serve to provide some indication of those infected with the virus, in many cases it would only give people a false sense of security.

AIDS AND SAFER SEX

What is safer sex?

Safer sex is any sexual practice that reduces the risk of HIV transmission or the transmission of other sexually associated diseases. We already know that any exchange of bodily fluids (particularly blood, semen or vaginal secretion) during sex is to be considered unsafe. So now we must learn how to appreciate sexual relationships without putting ourselves or our partner at risk.

When participating in any sexual activity, consider the following:

- [ ] Use a latex condom when involved in vaginal or anal intercourse and oral sex (fellatio). Even the pre-ejaculatory fluid from the male's Cowper's glands may contain the virus.
- [ ] Any oral involvement with the female sex organs (cunnilingus) should be considered a (low) risk activity. Vaginal secretions can carry HIV and if ingested could reach the bloodstream through cuts, wounds or abrasions in the mouth.
- [ ] Any activity that involves inserting the hands or tongue in the anus cavity should be considered risky. Even well-scrubbed hands will often have slight cuts and abrasions that could permit the transmission of the virus.
- [ ] Urine is another bodily fluid in which the virus has been found. Do not ingest urine.
- [ ] Under no circumstances should you share sex toys such as dildos, vibrators, etc.
- [ ] Any sexual activity that might involve blood exposure such as S/M (sadomasochistic practices) is a high risk activity. Direct contact with blood such as might be found on whips, ropes, handcuffs,

etc., should be considered a high risk.

☐ When using spermicides and lubricants look for those which contain the detergent **Nonoxynol-9**. Although it is yet undetermined whether Nonoxynol-9 can kill HIV inside the human body, the detergent has killed the virus in the laboratory, and is known to be effective against other sexually transmitted diseases such as the herpes virus, and the bacteria that causes gonorrhea and syphilis.

☐ Dry kissing, as opposed to 'French' kissing, is a safer sex practice. Deep kissing or 'French' kissing, which involves inserting the tongue into your partner's mouth, creates an exchange of saliva and should be considered at least a low risk activity. HIV has been found in saliva.

☐ Mutual masturbation, body massage and body-to-body rubbing are all considered safe practices. There has been no evidence to date of the virus in sweat or perspiration.

Remember: AIDS does not have to mean the end of sex. Safer sex guidelines will only work if they are widely known and practised accordingly. Talk openly with your friends and sexual partners about 'safer sex' practices and identify the risk factor accordingly. The following is a list of sexual activities that are considered to be NO RISK, LOW RISK, and HIGH RISK.

NO RISK:
☐ mutual masturbation
☐ social 'dry' kissing
☐ hugging
☐ massaging

☐ body to body contact where there are no breaks or abrasions in the skin

LOW RISK:
☐ cunnilingus (oral-vaginal contact)
☐ 'French' kissing . . . inserting the tongue into a partner's mouth
☐ vaginal or anal intercourse using a latex condom (spermicides further reduce the risk)
☐ fellatio (oral sex); inserting the penis in the mouth and not allowing semen to enter

HIGH RISK:
☐ vaginal or anal intercourse without using a condom
☐ inserting the hands or tongue into the anus cavity
☐ sharing sex toys such as dildos, vibrators, etc.
☐ S/M (sadomasochistic practices)

Are condoms a guarantee against AIDS?
While condoms are not an absolute guarantee against AIDS, they are the best preventive measure available other than sexual activities without the exchange of semen or blood, or abstinence (no sexual activity).

Researchers at the University of California, San Francisco have proven in laboratory tests that condoms can stop HIV. The virus cannot penetrate the condom material of latex rubber condoms unless the condoms are ruptured. Further research is being done to establish the degree of effectiveness of natural skin condoms as a barrier against the virus. Animal membrane condoms do not effectively reduce the risk of HIV infection as they are more permeable than latex condoms. It has also been clinically proven that condoms will help prevent the transmission of other sexually transmitted diseases including herpes simplex, gonorrhea and syphilis.

Regardless of precautions taken, all sexually active people with multiple partners are advised to exercise safer sex practices. The use of condoms is statistically considered 95% effective. Learn how to use a condom properly. See illustrations on page 75.

What are the best condoms to buy?

All condoms (prophylactics, safes, rubbers) must meet the standards established by the 'Medical Devices Regulations' set by the Canadian Food and Drug Act. However, Canada's largest distributor of condoms suggests that condoms should be purchased from retail outlets such as drug stores and purchasers should look to be sure the condoms they are buying have been 'electronically' tested by the manufacturer for maximum protection.

Condoms generally have a shelf life of five years under ideal conditions, but can begin to deteriorate slowly after a period of time. Condoms deteriorate as the result of heat, strong light and rough treatment. They should not be left in the sun or kept in glove compartments or billfolds for long periods, or stored in a place where they will be subject to direct sources of ultra violet light (fluorescent).

Your choice of condoms is a question of personal preference. Latex condoms as opposed to 'natural skin' condoms are recommended to reduce the risk of HIV infection. Natural skin condoms are more fragile and can be permeable to HIV. All condoms are available in a variety of shapes, sizes, colors and textures and can be lubricated or unlubricated. Do not have any hesitancy discussing your choice of condom with your doctor or local pharmacist.

Important: When using a condom, use only water-based lubricants. Do not use vaseline, mineral oil or any petroleum preparation. These will cause breakage. When additional lubrication is required, use a name brand surgical jelly. It is also recommended that spermicide foam or jelly be used in conjunction with condoms for maximum protection.

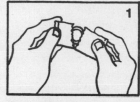

HOW TO USE A CONDOM PROPERLY

Remove condom from packaging very carefully to ensure condom texture is not damaged by long nails, rings or bracelets.

Pull the condom over the head of the erect penis. If the condom is not designed with a small receptacle end, leave about ½" space at the end of the condom. Squeeze end slightly to release air and prevent an air pocket. Air inside the condom can interfere with sensitivity and may cause condom breakage.
Slowly unroll condom until entire penis has been covered.

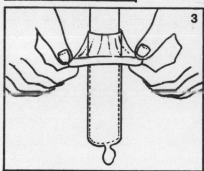

After ejaculation, slowly withdraw the penis, holding the condom rim to prevent spillage. Do not allow penis or condom to touch vagina after withdrawal. Use a new condom each time intercourse is repeated.

NOTE: To further reduce the risk of AIDS or other sexually transmitted diseases . . . wash the penis and surrounding area, preferably with soap and water. URINATE.

AIDS AND GOVERNMENT

Are immigrants with AIDS allowed into Canada?
No. In 1985, Canada added AIDS to the list of diseases (which includes tuberculosis, syphilis and leprosy) that can bar prospective immigrants from coming to this country. The federal government has indicated that there are no plans for mandatory AIDS testing of would-be immigrants. Instead of tests, Canada relies on the medical records of an applicant compiled in the country of origin, which may or may not include the AIDS test.

Health and Welfare Canada has three conditions concerning AIDS which it applies to newcomers:
a) A person diagnosed as having AIDS cannot be admitted;
b) Someone in whom some symptoms of AIDS are present, cannot be admitted;
c) A person with a medical history indicating the presence of HIV, but is medical stable, may qualify for a 'conditional' admission.

NOTE: In United States effective December 1, 1987, all immigrants and refugees wishing to become permanent U.S. residents are required to take a test for exposure to HIV. Those testing positive will not be allowed to become U.S. residents. It is estimated approximately 660,000 people a year will be tested under this public health service regulation.

What is the Canadian Government doing to avert an AIDS epidemic?
In 1982, the Laboratory Centre for Disease Control at Health and Welfare Canada began a series of activities in response to AIDS. As the disease, the

issues and the concerns grew, so did the activities and the amount of funding dedicated to AIDS programs.

In 1986, the Canadian government pledged $39 million to be spent over a five year period in the fight against AIDS. Of this money, $26.5 million is being spent on research programs and laboratory testing facilities. The balance will be used for community support programs and public and professional education programs.

In July 1987, the Federal Centre for AIDS was established. Based in Ottawa, the Centre is part of the Health Protection Branch of Health and Welfare Canada.

Briefly, the Federal Centre for AIDS traces the course of AIDS and HIV infection in Canada; supports the search for new AIDS drugs and vaccines; assists health and social services to deal with AIDS and HIV infection; educates Canadians about AIDS; and fulfills Canada's responsibilities in the international fight against AIDS.

The Canadian Public Health Association was awarded major federal government funding of 3.7 million over five years to establish a National AIDS Education and Awareness Program. It works in close collaboration with the Federal Centre for AIDS.

There are currently 25 community AIDS groups (see listing at the back of this book) that are partially funded by the federal government. These committees provide a variety of services in their communities, from counselling AIDS patients, to the production of educational materials directed at high risk groups.

The Federal Centre for AIDS works closely with the provinces through the Federal/Provincial/Territorial Advisory Committee on AIDS to plan and coordinate activities of the two levels of government in dealing with all aspects of AIDS.

Health and Welfare Canada established the National Advisory Committee on AIDS (NAC-AIDS), now in its fifth year. NAC-AIDS provides expert scientific advice and recommendations to the Minister of Health and Welfare Canada on a variety of AIDS issues.

What is the World Health Organization (WHO) doing about AIDS?

The World Health Organization (WHO), headquartered in Geneva, Switzerland, has a membership of 166 countries (May 1986) and works co-operatively with its member governments in their efforts to develop health manpower, streamline health services, control communicable diseases, promote family health (including mother and child care, family planning, nutrition and health education) and strengthens environmental health. The organization promotes biomedical and health services through some 800 collaborating research centres in different parts of the world.

In November 1986, the director-general of the World Health Organization announced that in the same spirit and with the same dedication to global purpose with which WHO undertook the fight against smallpox, WHO is now committed to the more urgent, difficult and complex challenge of global AIDS prevention and control.

The numbers of reported cases of AIDS and countries reporting AIDS has increased dramatically. In December 1982, 711 AIDS cases were reported to WHO from 18 countries; by April 1987, 44,825 AIDS cases were reported from 91 countries representing all continents. As of March 1988 the total number of AIDS cases reported to WHO was 80,912 from 129 countries. Reticence in the reporting of cases from some areas, combined with under-recognition of AIDS and unreported cases represents only a fraction of the total cases to date; these are estimated to be in excess of 100,000. The World Health Organization estimates that between five and ten million persons are currently infected with HIV.

Despite rapid advances in the early phases of vaccine development, a vaccine suitable for large-scale use is highly unlikely to become available prior to the mid-1990s according to WHO sources. The WHO strategy therefore is to serve as an international co-ordinator and to concentrate immediate efforts on communications and education, developing programs with their member governments to:

a) develop and strengthen health promotion approaches leading to sustained changes in global sexual behavior;

b) develop and strengthen blood transfusion systems to ensure appropriate collection, screening and use of blood and providing counselling and medical evaluation services (pre- and post-donation);

c) ensure that blood products are produced in a manner which eliminates the risk of HIV transmission;

d) ensure the use of sterile needles, syringes and other skin-piercing instruments;

e) prevent HIV transmission through organ and semen donations;

f) develop, implement and evaluate ways to reduce HIV transmission from infected mother to child;

g) collaborate with institutions internationally to develop, test, produce and deliver drugs and other therapeutic agents to prevent the transmission of the virus;

h) develop, test and produce an AIDS vaccine;

i) to reduce the impact of HIV infection on individuals, groups and society.

All of the above programs being undertaken by WHO are extensive and extremely elaborate in implementation. These Special AIDS Programs have a budget in 1987 of more than $48 million (U.S.) which will be doubled in 1988. WHO is also providing technical assistance and financial support to member governments in the planning, design, and evaluation of their national AIDS programs. Direct financial aid to 50 countries requiring assistance for their AIDS programs is estimated at $18.75 million dollars in 1987.

WHO program funding comes from voluntary contributions from member states. Canada is a major contributor.

AIDS AND WOMEN

Why should women be concerned about AIDS?

In North America, most people with AIDS are men. As of March 7, 1988, there have been only 82 cases of women with AIDS in Canada. However, because AIDS is a sexually transmitted disease, women can become infected and infect others. They can carry the virus and pass it to their babies before or at birth, or, in rare instances, through breast-feeding.

While it is possible for women to become infected with AIDS, it is also easy for them to protect themselves from the disease. To prevent the spread of the disease, to understand its effects and reduce their risk of exposure, women should know all the facts about AIDS.

Which groups of women are most at risk?

The HIV is transmitted in four known ways:
□ through sexual intercourse with an infected person
□ through sharing contaminated needles or syringes
□ through transfusion of infected blood or blood products
□ from an infected mother to her baby, before or at birth, or in rare instances through breast milk

Certain groups of women are at greater risk of exposure to the virus and should take precautions. They are:
□ Women whose sexual partners have AIDS or are carriers of HIV
□ Prostitutes
□ Women who have multiple sexual contacts

☐ Women whose sexual partners are bisexual or have had homosexual contacts since 1980 (when it is estimated the first AIDS cases began to develop in Canada)
☐ Women who are intravenous drug abusers and share needles and other equipment
☐ Women whose sexual partners abuse drugs
☐ Women who received or whose sexual partners received many blood or blood product transfusion between 1980 and November 1985 (when the Red Cross began screening blood)
☐ Women who have been artificially inseminated with donor semen. If the donor's blood was not tested for the HIV antibodies, the semen could carry the virus and the women are at a very slight risk of infection.

How can women protect themselves against AIDS?
The surest way to protect yourself is to avoid sexual contact with:
☐ bisexual men or men who have had a homosexual contact since 1980
☐ persons who abuse intravenous drugs
☐ multiple partners or with persons who have had multiple partners
☐ anyone whose history and health status is unknown

If you do have sex other than in a mutually monogamous relationship:
☐ Insist that your partner use a condom. This will greatly reduce some of the risk. Condoms can also protect you from other sexually-transmitted diseases such as syphilis and gonorrhea.

☐ Don't indulge in any activities in which semen or blood enters the vagina, anus or mouth.

☐ If you want to be especially careful, abstain from "deep-kissing". The risk is very slight, but HIV has been found in small amounts in the saliva of infected people and might get into another person's bloodstream through cuts or sores in the mouth.

☐ Don't abuse drugs. If you are an I.V. (intravenous) drug user, never share needles or syringes. Assistance for drug abusers is available from your local health agency.

☐ Prostitutes risk exposure to the virus. Counselling and information are available from Sexually Transmitted Disease (STD) clinics, family doctors and from the various AIDS groups across Canada, listed in the back of this book.

What about artificial insemination?
If you are planning artificial insemination, check with your doctor to ensure that the donor's blood has been tested and does not contain the HIV antibody.

How can women with the HIV antibody protect others?
If you have AIDS or HIV antibodies in your blood, you are very likely to be infectious. To reduce the risk of passing the virus to someone else:

☐ Tell your sexual partner.

☐ Insist that your sexual partner use latex condoms.

☐ During your menstrual period, abstain from sexual activities that would expose your partner to your blood.

□ Wrap and carefully dispose of any blood-soiled products (napkins and tampons).

□ Don't share razors, toothbrushes or other implements which might be contaminated with your blood. Avoid any activities that would expose people or equipment to your blood, such as electrolysis, tattooing and ear piercing.

□ HIV has also been found in breast milk. If you have a baby, consult your doctor before deciding to breast-feed.

□ Inform anyone who provides you with health care and may come into contact with your blood – such as doctors, dentists or nurses – so they can take adequate precaution.

Is a woman who lives in a household with someone who has AIDS at risk?
It depends whether the contact is casual, care-giving or sexual. With casual contact – even daily – there's no risk. Extensive studies of families of AIDS patients have found not one case of the disease being spread through everyday contact. Not one case of AIDS has been transmitted by casual contact from parent to child, from child to brother or sister, or from child to parent. There's no danger in sharing bathrooms, food, kitchenware or clothes. There's no risk from touching, hugging, or kissing without the exchange of saliva.

For men and women who give personal care to someone who has AIDS and may come in contact with the infected person's blood or other body fluids, there's a very slight risk. To prevent the virus from entering the bloodstream through cuts or sores on their hands, they should wear plastic, disposable gloves and wash their hands thoroughly when handling the bodily fluids of AIDS patients. It would also be helpful to read **AIDS and the Health Care Worker** beginning on page 115.

If a woman has a sexual relationship with the person who has AIDS, the risk is much greater. She and her partner should take safer sex precautions and avoid pregnancy. They may want to contact their doctor or local public health unit for counselling.

Many of the health care workers and laboratory staff caring for AIDS patients are women. Are they at risk?
Only health care workers and laboratory staff who handle body fluids, such as blood, semen, feces and urine of AIDS patients, are at any risk. They should follow the infection control practices and procedures recommended in their institutions as outlined by federal guidelines and HIV will not have the opportunity to enter their bloodstreams.

Several hundred health care workers worldwide have accidentally pricked themselves with needles contaminated with the virus. A small number of them have been found to have the HIV antibodies in their bloodstream. However, only a very few of them are not members of a high risk group and, as no consistent pre-testing was done, even those few could have been exposed to the virus before their accidents.

Are lesbians likely to get AIDS?
No. There is no evidence of AIDS being transmitted

from an infected woman to another woman through sexual contact. However, contact with menstrual blood, which may contain HIV, should be avoided.

There is one incident reported in the *Annals of Internal Medicine* (Dec. '86) of a lesbian with AIDS. This was a letter submitted by a doctor citing one case of a lesbian who had claimed to have contracted AIDS from her female partner. This claim has not been substantiated according to the Centres for Disease Control in Atlanta, and it may be that the virus was contracted at some earlier time from a male partner.

Should women be tested for the HIV antibodies?
If you do not engage in high risk behaviors, it is unlikely that you have been exposed to HIV and do not need to be tested.

If you have been involved in a high-risk activity, or think you may have been exposed to the virus, you may want to be tested. This is particularly important if you are considering having a child. (Although there is no test available that will identify the virus, the HIV antibody test will tell you if you have been exposed to HIV).

Don't make a blood donation in order to have the blood test. If you want to be tested, contact your doctor or your local AIDS group.

If the test shows that you have the virus antibodies in your blood, this does not mean you have AIDS. It does mean that you have been exposed to HIV, you are likely to be infectious, you should take safer sex precautions, and should consider contraception.

Recently in the United States, voluntary testing has been recommended for women prior to marriage or pregnancy, but only if they have a history of high risk activities, and are from urban areas with a relatively high rate of HIV infection. Such voluntary testing in Canada is now being considered by various jurisdictions.

INFORMATION FOR
PARENTS AND TEACHERS

How many children have AIDS?

The number of children with AIDS in North America is still relatively small. As of March 7, 1988 there have been 33 cases of children (under 15 years of age) diagnosed with AIDS in Canada, of whom 20 have died.

In the United States (as of March 7, 1988) there have been 865 recorded cases of children with AIDS (under 13 years of age).

How did these children get AIDS?

The majority of children who have AIDS acquired the disease from their infected mothers before birth.

Some children contracted AIDS from the transfusion of infected blood or blood products.

In other words, and this is a very important point, – not one case of AIDS in children was caused by casual contact. Not one case was caused by touching, biting, hugging, playing, or by sharing food or utensils.

Hopefully, with the screening of blood products and prenatal screening of mothers at risk for HIV infection, pediatric AIDS will remain rare in Canada. Unfortunately, in some major cities in the United States and other countries there are many women of child-bearing age who are infected. AIDS in children will result from this spread.

Are children at risk if they are in contact with infected children?

If such contact is casual, no, they are not at risk.

AIDS is caused by a virus called HIV (Human Immunodeficiency Virus). In order for the virus to spread, it has to pass into another person's bloodstream. There are only four ways in which this can happen:

- [ ] through certain kinds of sexual contact;
- [ ] through sharing contaminated needles or syringes;
- [ ] through the transfusion of infected blood or blood products;
- [ ] from an infected mother to her baby before or at birth.

Unless a child is involved in any of the first three activities with an infected person, he or she is not at risk.

Extensive studies of families of AIDS patients have found not one case of the disease being spread through everyday contact. This is an important finding when you consider the amount of personal contact families have. They hug and kiss each other. They play, eat, often bathe and sleep together. They share bathrooms, food, kitchenware and clothes. And parents regularly clean up their children's vomit, blood, feces and urine. Yet not one case of AIDS has been transmitted from parent to child (except in pregnancy), from child to brother or sister. Only one case of spread from child to parent is thought to have occurred, resulting from extensive exposure of the parent to the child's blood.

Are students at risk from teachers with AIDS?
Unless a student is involved in any of the first two risk activities outlined in the previous question and answer, he or she is not at risk.

Will teachers, cooks or other school staff with AIDS be able to work in school?

Yes. Since there is no risk to others in the workplace, infected staff will continue to work as long as their doctors say they are well enough.

Will parents and teachers be told if there is a child or member of school staff with AIDS in their community?

No. AIDS – unlike chicken pox, for example – is not a contagious disease, so it would not be necessary. This information, like any other medical information, is held in the strictest confidence. It will only be discussed between the patient, (the patient's parents in the instance of children), his or her doctor and the local medical officer of health.

Will children with AIDS be allowed in school?

Yes, they will, but each case will be individually assessed. As already noted, there is no danger to other children from everyday contact with an infected child in school, home, or at play.

Under certain circumstances, however, the medical officer of health may decide to keep a child out of school. Usually, this will be for the protection of the child with AIDS; for example, if the child is too ill to attend school, or vulnerable to infections.

In rare cases, the medical officer of health may decide to be extra cautious by excluding a child whose condition or behavior may pose even the slightest risk to others. If a child bites, for example, or lacks bladder or bowel control, he or she may be withdrawn from school – even though body fluids such as saliva and urine have never been shown to transmit the virus.

It is important to mention that teachers and other school staff should be aware of blood precautions (e.g. handling blood spills, etc.) and are advised to read **AIDS and the Health Care Worker** (see page 115).

How can young people be protected from infection?
The same way as adults. The surest way to avoid infection is to refrain from risk activities. If any person is involved in one of the risk activities previously outlined, here are some of the things that can be done:

☐ Before young people participate in any sexual activity they should be fully informed about sexually-transmitted diseases (STD's). Many responsible parents, once reluctant, are now encouraging sex education in our schools, beginning as early as the elementary levels.

STD and AIDS education will be provided by many school boards and provinces in the coming year, in an effort to help students understand AIDS and its prevention. This education in school and in the home is a vital part of teaching sexual development, responsibility and decision-making skills.

☐ Children should also be taught the hazards of drug abuse. In particular the dangers of sharing drug paraphernalia, including needles or syringes, which dramatically increases the risk of infection with HIV or hepatitis.

AIDS AND

THE WORKPLACE

Can people be fired because they have AIDS or are infected with HIV?

People who have AIDS or who are infected with HIV are not a health risk to co-workers so there is no medical reason to dismiss them. There is legislation in all provinces to protect Canadians from illegal discrimination.

In the province of Ontario, for example, the Ontario Human Rights Code prohibits discrimination in employment based on a disabling condition.

If a person were fired because he or she either:

☐ has AIDS
☐ is infected with HIV, or
☐ is suspected of having AIDS – there could be a violation of the employee's rights.

An employee who feels that his or her rights have been violated may file a complaint with their local Human Rights Commission. In addition, the employee may be able to sue the employer for wrongful dismissal.

Can I get AIDS from an infected co-worker?

There have been no cases of AIDS being spread in the workplace through non-sexual contact with persons with AIDS. There is no evidence that being in the same office, working on the same assembly line or using the same equipment as someone with AIDS – even for a long period of time – puts you at any risk of becoming infected with the virus.

Is there any risk in using cups, telephones, locker rooms or other facilities that are also used by a co-

worker who has AIDS or who has been infected with HIV?

HIV cannot be transmitted through air, water or food, or by touching the skin of a person with AIDS, or by touching any object handled, touched or breathed on by a person with AIDS. People can't get AIDS from public toilets, drinking fountains, telephones, public transportation or swimming pools.

Extensive studies of families of persons with AIDS have not found one case of the disease spread through sharing common facilities.

Can I get AIDS from eating in a restaurant where someone handling the food has AIDS?

No. No cases of AIDS have been transmitted through food preparation or food handling. The Human Immunodeficiency Virus is very fragile and survives for only a short time outside the human body. Even if the virus were present, it would be killed by the standard public health cleaning practices required of all restaurants or businesses handling food.

Are personal service workers at risk if the customer has AIDS or is infected with HIV?

There has never been a case of a personal service worker becoming infected with HIV from non-sexual contact with a client or customer.

The risk of being exposed to the virus depends on the type of service performed. There is a potential risk only if the worker comes into contact with the client's blood and there is an opportunity for the virus to enter the worker's bloodstream.

Personal service workers such as hairdressers, barbers, beauticians, cosmetologists, manicurists and pedicurists may have close personal contact with clients, but they rarely come into contact with blood, and therefore have little risk of exposure.

Personal service workers who:
☐ pierce ears
☐ produce tattoos
☐ use acupuncture
☐ provide electrolysis
☐ may come into contact with blood and, therefore, could be at slight risk.

To protect against any infections, all personal service workers should follow good hygiene practices. They should:
☐ wash their hands thoroughly
☐ cover any cuts or sores on their hands
☐ clean their equipment according to recommended procedures
☐ use disposable equipment where appropriate
☐ clean anything that has been contaminated with blood using rubbing alcohol or a bleach solution (1 part household, chlorine bleach – such as Javex – to 9 parts water).

These precautions will protect against hepatitis B and other bloodborne infections – including HIV.

If a personal service worker has AIDS or is infected with HIV, are his or her customers at risk?
There has never been a case of someone becoming infected with HIV from non-sexual contact with a barber, hairdresser or other personal care worker. The good hygiene practices described for workers also protect customers.

Are health care workers who are caring for persons with AIDS at risk?

Health care workers and laboratory staff who handle body fluids such as blood, semen, feces and urine of AIDS patients run a slight risk of coming into contact with HIV. To protect themselves, they should follow the infection control practices and procedures recommended in their institutions so that the virus will not have the opportunity to enter their bloodstreams.

Studies have shown that, even in cases where health care workers have accidentally stuck themselves with needles contaminated with blood infected with the virus, the chance of becoming infected is very small – well over 100 times less than with hepatitis B.

More information can be found in **AIDS and the Health Care Worker**, beginning on page 115.

Are patients at risk if the health care worker is infected with HIV?

Infection control procedures in hospitals or clinics that protect health care workers also protect patients. In most hospital situations, there is little opportunity for a patient to be exposed to the blood of a health care worker and, therefore, there is very little risk. During invasive procedures, such as surgery or kidney dialysis, precautions are already in place to prevent bloodborne infections such as hepatitis B, and they would also protect against AIDS.

Are ambulance drivers, police officers, firefighters

and other emergency workers at risk of HIV infection?

HIV infection is not spread by touching, carrying or holding a person who is infected. Non-sexual contact is not risky.

However, ambulance or other emergency personnel will likely come into contact with blood and other bodily fluids in emergency situations. Even if these fluids contain the virus, the risk of infection is slight. There have been no cases of anyone becoming infected with the virus from providing emergency care for an infected person.

To protect against any infection, emergency workers should follow strict infection control practices in caring for emergency victims. They should:
□ wash their hands thoroughly
□ clean their equipment according to recommended procedures
If they are likely to come into contact with blood or bodily fluids, they should:
□ wear plastic, disposable gloves.
□ cover any cuts or sores on their hands
□ clean any contaminated surfaces with a chlorine bleach solution
These simple precautions will protect them from hepatitis B and other bloodborne infections – including AIDS.

Although very small quantities of HIV have been found in saliva, there have been no cases of virus infection transmitted through saliva. Emergency workers who regularly give mouth-to-mouth resuscitation or CPR to victims may protect themselves from a variety of diseases by using a specially designed mouthpiece. However, the risk of infection is so slight that no one should hesitate to give emergency mouth-to-mouth resuscitation without a mouthpiece.

How should an employer treat an employee who has AIDS?

As long as the employee is able to perform the essential duties of his or her job, the employer's approach should be the same as with any other employee.

At certain stages in the illness, the employee may be too ill to work. When this happens, or when the workplace becomes dangerous to the employee's health, the approach to the person with AIDS should be the same as with any other employee who has a serious illness. Whenever possible, attempts should be made to adjust work requirements to accommodate the person's health.

The employer should be sensitive to the fact that ongoing employment for someone who has a life-threatening illness is important, and may help to prolong the employee's life, by providing a supportive and caring environment.

Does an employer have the right to know if an employee has AIDS?

Since AIDS cannot be transmitted by everyday contact in the workplace, there is no need for employers, co-workers, neighbors or anyone who does not have intimate sexual contact with the person with AIDS to know. The person with AIDS has *a legal right to privacy and confidentiality*. An employer can only request medical information from an employee that is relevant to his or her job. An employer can only confirm this information with a physician with the employee's expressed consent.

Should an employer request blood testing for employees?

Employers do not have the right to insist on mandatory blood testing. Testing might be considered for health care workers who, through an injury in the workplace, have been exposed to infected blood or bodily fluids. In those cases, testing is for the benefit of the employee and should be voluntary.

In other work situations, there's usually no reason to test employees. Some exceptions that have been discussed are military personnel (screening of recruits is currently being done in the United States, but not in Canada) and in foreign service development workers who may go to areas of the world with high rates of HIV infection.

Available blood tests identify antibodies to HIV, which indicate that a person has been exposed to the virus. If the virus antibodies are found in a person's blood, it doesn't necessarily mean that a person has AIDS or will go on to develop AIDS. Nor does it mean the person is immune to AIDS. (Usually antibodies protect a person from a disease, but this is not the case with HIV antibodies.)

If antibodies are found, it simply means that, at some time in the past, the virus has entered the person's bloodstream. It is currently unclear what percentage of people who have the antibodies will actually develop AIDS. Some people have the virus in their bloodstream for a number of year and never develop symptoms of AIDS. Others develop AIDS after the virus has been present in the blood for a few months. Still others take several years to develop AIDS.

What should employers do about AIDS?

Employers should set an example for their employees and refrain from discrimination. They should also take action to prevent discrimination among employees in the workplace.

Employers should help employees become informed. General information about AIDS is available from federal and provincial ministries of health, the Canadian Public Health Association, your local public health boards and from the various AIDS groups throughout Canada listed in this book on pages 131–135.

This book is also available at special discounts for quantity purchases by employers who may wish to distribute it to their employees. Information concerning quantity purchases can be obtained by contacting the Canadian Public Health Association or Summerhill Press.

Employers should distribute information and provide educational sessions that will help employees understand AIDS and HIV and how it is transmitted. More knowledge will mean less fear, less discrimination and greater productivity.

What should unions do about AIDS?

Unions are a powerful force in communication and education and can help their members get accurate information about AIDS. They can also help prevent discrimination in the workplace. Union groups are forming committees to educate union leaders, staff and members about AIDS.

AIDS AND DENTISTRY

Should Canadians be concerned about contracting AIDS while receiving dental treatment?
There are no reports of Canadians being infected with HIV while undergoing dental care. As has previously been explained in this book, infected blood is the major route of transmissions. In dental procedures this is not a danger since the only blood which patients would be exposed to is their own.

Can I become infected with HIV while sitting in the dental waiting room?
No. All evidence suggests that the HIV is not transferred via the casual social contact which occurs in dental waiting rooms or any doctors' offices. Similarly, the virus is not spread via newspapers, magazines, pens or pencils.

Is it possible for infected blood from one patient to be spread to another from dirty needles or instruments?
For many years, dentists have administered local anaesthetics with disposable needles. Once the appropriate level of anaesthesia (freezing) has been obtained, the needles are safely discarded and never used on subsequent patients. Therefore, in dentistry, infected needles are not a route of HIV transmission.

Dentists are aware of the need to effectively sterilize and disinfect, between patients. All instruments used in the mouth including the dental drill go through this procedure after each patient. In addition, the dental staff use a variety of techniques to ensure that contaminated blood does not remain on

working surfaces, X-ray machines, light-handles, etc.
These measures ensure that infected blood which
may cover instruments or be spilled in the dental
treatment room does not remain to contaminate
other patients.

**If there is little risk of exposure to HIV in the dental
office, why are more and more dentists wearing
gloves and masks?**
Gloves, face masks and protective glasses are
known as barrier precautions. Dentists have real-
ized that by using these precautions they protect
patients from diseases especially colds which they
or their staff may have, while at the same time pro-
tecting themselves from viruses and bacteria in the
blood and saliva of patients. Gloves not only isolate
the dentist's hands from patient's blood but also
ensure that any blood from cuts or abrasions on
the dentist's fingers will not spread to the patient's
mouth.

Patients should not feel intimidated or discrimi-
nated against when these barrier precautions are
used. On the contrary, they should appreciate that
the dental staff is serious about reducing the spread
of disease.

**Although AIDS is spread mainly by infected blood
and semen, is it possible that the virus could be
transferred by saliva and by saliva contaminated
dental instruments?**
HIV has been found in saliva, however all authorities do not consider that saliva is a route of transmission. In addition, the sterilization techniques used

to remove blood from dental instruments would destroy all traces of saliva.

If an AIDS patient is in the terminal phase of the illness with only a few weeks to live, is dental treatment necessary?

The mouth, which even in the healthy patient contains thousands of microorganisms, is a route by which immune compromised AIDS patients may obtain a severe, perhaps fatal opportunistic infection. Therefore for ARC and AIDS patients, the maintenance of good oral hygiene is an essential function of the dental team. While it is unlikely that extensive, expensive restorative dentistry would be justified for a dying AIDS patient, such an individual is entitled to be treated for acute oral pain, or infection.

I have heard that some of the signs of AIDS are seen in the mouth. Is this true?

Yes. Kaposi's sarcoma (a tumor of blood vessels) – one of the signs of AIDS – often occurs in the mouth. Its presence in the mouth may be the first definite proof that the patient has AIDS. Thrush – a fungal infection – causes thick milk-like plaques to form on the tongue, roof of the mouth, and inside of the cheeks. Thrush is an opportunistic infection which is commonly associated with ARC and AIDS. Unusual white areas on the sides of the tongue, failure of mouth or gum infections to respond to normal treatment, or delayed healing after dental surgery, may all suggest the presence of a defective immune system which could be due to an HIV infection. Thus, the dentist may be the first health care worker to recognize that the patient could have AIDS, or that there are sufficient oral signs present to justify medical tests for a possible HIV infection.

Should AIDS patients be required to attend special dental clinics, so that patients without AIDS will be safe in going to their private dentists?

As previously explained, the chance of an HIV infection being acquired during dental treatment is so slim that patients need not be alarmed if their dentist is caring for AIDS patients. In some instances, the AIDS patient may be so acutely ill that essential dental treatment is best performed in a hospital based dental unit where the necessary medical facilities are available if required.

It is estimated that up to 50,000 Canadians may already be infected with HIV. The majority of these people feel well, look healthy, and do not know that they are infected. However, they are capable of spreading the disease. Dentists are aware of this. That is why they wear barrier precautions and sterilize instruments to ensure that diseases including AIDS are not spread via dental treatment or the office environment. This is one reason why special dental clinics for HIV infected individuals are not necessary to protect the general public.

Is it important that I answer the dentist's questions regarding any recent changes in my health status, or whether or not I have HIV infection or AIDS?

Yes. Your answers to these questions are very important. Dentists are trained to recognize that certain changes in your health may be significant, and for your own good be worthy of additional investigation by your physician. Infections with HIV, especially those which have progressed to ARC and AIDS, are accompanied by changes in the immune system which may affect dental treatment. Therefore, it is important for the dentist to know if an HIV infection is present, the extent of its progression, and to consult with your physician to determine appropriate dental care.

Have patients with AIDS been refused dental treatment?

It is unfortunate but true that some AIDS patients have been denied dental care. Dentists are within their rights to refuse to treat any new patient, although they have a moral and ethical responsibility to ensure that all patients whom they decline to treat (for whatever reasons) are referred to willing and capable colleagues.

Should dentists or their staff with HIV infection or AIDS stop practicing?

The dentist or staff members who may be infected with HIV need not stop treating patients because the barrier precautions (gloves, masks, eyeglasses) which they wear will protect patients. If the disease progresses from ARC and then to AIDS, the infected dentist or staff member may no longer have the mental and physical skills to perform in a competent professional manner, and will have to retire from active practice.

I know that AIDS is basically a sexually transmitted disease, and that it is unlikely to be spread during dental treatment. Nevertheless, I am concerned that my children could be at risk attending the orthodontist's busy office, or having wisdom teeth removed by an oral surgeon. Who could respond to my concerns?
You should ask the treating dentist (specialist or general practitioner) to answer your questions, and to show you what precautions are being taken to prevent the spread of diseases such as HIV infection.

How do I know that my dentist is familiar with AIDS?
The Canadian Dental Association has sent all dentists information on AIDS. This national organization has made recommendations which will assist dentists in treating AIDS patients. The recommendations will be updated as more knowledge of the disease is obtained. Dentists wishing answers to specific questions are encouraged to: Contact the Provincial or National Dental Associations, read professional journals, and attend continuing education programs on AIDS and other infectious diseases.

AIDS AND THE

HEALTH CARE WORKER

Health care workers (HCWs), who come into contact either with persons with AIDS or with their body fluids, may be concerned about possible infection with Human Immuno-deficiency Virus (HIV). Patients who do not have AIDS may also be concerned that they could become infected through contact with health care workers who are caring for persons with AIDS.

While AIDS is not a highly contagious disease, the con-cern about possible transmission of infection gives health care facilities an opportunity to review and reinforce infec-tion control procedures. The following information sum-marizes infection control procedures that are effective in dealing with all bloodborne infections, including AIDS.

What is the risk of transmission of HIV to health care workers?

The Human Immunodeficiency Virus (HIV) is found in the blood and bodily fluids of an infected person and is primarily a sexually-transmitted agent. Although the epidemiology of AIDS is similar to that of hepatitis B, AIDS is much less contagious. The risk of a health care worker acquiring the virus in health care settings is extremely small.

In fact, nowhere in the world has a health care worker acquired AIDS from caring for someone with AIDS. Seven different studies have been done on a total of 1,758 health care workers who accidentally pricked themselves with needles contaminated with the virus. Some of them have been followed for as long as three years. As of the end of December 1986, none of them has developed AIDS.

In one specific case, a nurse in England acciden-tally injected herself with a large quantity of blood from someone with AIDS. Although she had some transient symptoms and developed the HIV antibodies, she has not developed AIDS.

What is the risk of transmission of HIV or other opportunistic infections to pregnant health care workers?

Persons with the HIV infection are sometimes also infected with *Cytomegalovirus* (CMV), *Epstein Barr virus* (EBV) and *hepatitis B virus* (HBV). While these viruses are possible causes of congenital infections, the risk of HCWs acquiring these infections from persons with AIDS or other patients is very small; and the risk to pregnant HCWs is no greater than for anyone else. Since there is no evidence of increased risk of infection in working with persons with AIDS, the transfer of pregnant HCWs to other work is not required. Pregnant women working with patients known or suspected of having CMV should be aware of the risk of infection, and the protective effect of standard hygienic techniques.

What is the risk of a patient acquiring HIV infection in a hospital setting?

There has never been a case of a patient becoming infected with HIV through exposure in a health care setting. However, HCWs should be aware that patients are concerned about infection and, in order to reassure them, HCWs should demonstrate a high level of professional competence and attention to hygienic techniques.

For the HCW who has a positive HIV antibody test but is otherwise well, procedures that prevent the transmission of any bloodborne infection will protect patients and co-workers from acquiring the virus from the HCW.

How can transmission of the Human Immunodeficiency Virus in health care settings be prevented?
EDUCATION: All HCWs, including students and housestaff, should be instructed in the epidemiology, modes of transmission and prevention of the virus infection.

PRECAUTIONS: Precautions which prevent the transmission of other bloodborne infectious diseases will also protect against HIV infection.

To prevent transmission of all bloodborne infections, including AIDS, the following procedures should be taken routinely:

1. HANDLING SHARPS
☐ Sharp items (needles, scalpel blades, lancets and other sharp instruments) contaminated with blood should be considered potentially infectious and be handled with extraordinary care to prevent accidental puncture injuries.
☐ Disposable syringes and needles, scalpel blades and other sharp items should be placed in rigid-walled, puncture-resistant containers placed as close as practical to the area in which the "sharps" are used. Needles should not be resheathed, bent, broken, removed from syringes or otherwise manipulated by hand as such actions increase the risk of skin punctures.

2. EXPOSURE TO BLOOD AND OTHER BODY FLUIDS
☐ HCWs should use protection appropriate to the

amount of exposure anticipated.

☐ GLOVES should be worn when handling items soiled with blood or equipment contaminated with blood or other body fluids. Gloves should also be worn during procedures when hands are likely to become soiled with blood.

☐ GOWNS should be worn when the HCWs clothing may become soiled with blood or bodily fluids.

☐ MASKS should be worn by HCWs who have direct and sustained contact with a coughing patient or with an incubated patient when suction is employed to clear the airway. Masks should be worn by coughing patients when they leave their room.

☐ EYE PROTECTION (goggles) should be worn in situations where spattering with blood or other body fluids might occur, such as endoscopic examinations and some dental procedures. The goggles should be the type designed to protect eyes against chemical splash hazards.

☐ CONTAMINATED SURFACES (floors, walls, etc.) should be decontaminated with a 0.6% sodium hypochlorite (Javex) 1 in 10 solution (1 part Javex to 9 parts water), and left for 20 minutes or until initially well-moistened surfaces are dry.

3. **PERSONAL HYGIENE PRACTISES**

☐ Hands should be washed immediately after removing gloves and gowns, after contact with blood or body fluids, and before and after leaving the room of an infectious patient. Avoid abrasive soaps and the use of brushes which may cause breaks in the skin.

☐ Splashes of blood to the face should be rinsed gently with water to minimize the risk of infection through the mucous membranes of the eyes and mouth.

4. TRANSPORTING AND CONTAINING POTENTIALLY INFECTIOUS MATERIAL

☐ Disposable items should be bagged and labelled as 'infectious waste' for autoclaving and/or disposal.

☐ Contaminated linen should be bagged and labelled accordingly.

☐ HCWs providing care in the home for a person with AIDS should wrap blood or fluid soiled disposable items carefully before putting them in the garbage.

☐ Laboratory specimens should be limited to those essential for patient care.

☐ Laboratory specimens transported within an institution should be labelled with appropriate biohazard symbols indicating blood and body fluid precautions are required. Specimens should be place in a waterproof bag or container for transportation. If the outside of the container is contaminated with blood or body secretions, it should be cleaned with an appropriate disinfectant (e.g. sodium hypochlorite at a dilution of one part household bleach to nine parts of water) and left for twenty minutes or until the initially well-moistened surface is dry.

☐ Laboratory specimens transported between institutions should be placed in a leak-proof bag or container, surrounded by absorbent padding and placed in a durable (e.g. metal) sealed outer container. For the information of those transporting and handling the specimen, the container should be clearly labelled with appropriate biohazard symbols requiring blood and body fluid precautions.

5. **PRECAUTIONS FOR LABORATORY PERSONNEL HANDLING POTENTIALLY INFECTIOUS MATERIAL**

☐ Laboratory specimens should be handled only by personnel who are knowledgeable in sterile techniques and biological safety procedures.

☐ Specimens which are leaking or contaminated on the outside of the container should not be accepted.

☐ Laboratory workers should not drink, smoke, store food or apply cosmetics in work areas.

☐ Gloves should be worn during procedures that may result in direct contact with potentially infectious materials; used gloved should be autoclaved with other laboratory waste before disposal.

☐ Never mouth-pipet. Use mechanical pipetting devices for manipulation of all liquids.

☐ During procedures which may create aerosols (e.g. tissue grinding, vigorous mixing, sonicating), a class B or class C biological safety cabinet should be used.

☐ Centrifuging should be done in a safety centrifuge, with an enclosed autoclavable head, or in a safety cabinet.

☐ After any spill of potentially infectious material and at the end of work activities, laboratory work surfaces should be decontaminated with a 0.6% sodiumhypochlorite (Javex) solution (1.9 dilution), and left for twenty minutes or until initially well-moistened surfaces are dry.

☐ All laboratory items and waste should be decontaminated by autoclaving before reuse or disposal.

☐ Protective clothing should be removed before leaving the laboratory.

☐ Hands should be washed with soap and water following completion of laboratory activities and before leaving the laboratory.

6. SPECIAL PRECAUTIONS TO BE TAKEN WITH PATIENTS

☐ Routine screening of patients or HCWs for the HIV antibody or hepatitis B infections is not recommended.

☐ Blood and body fluids from any patient – regardless of the diagnosis, should be handled with care and attention to good hygiene practices.

☐ Isolation of a person with AIDS in a single room is not necessary unless the patient is too ill to maintain good hygiene practices, is coughing, has diarrhea or has behavior problems. However, blood and bodily fluid precautions should be followed even though the patient is not isolated.

☐ The bodies of deceased persons with AIDS should be placed in a body bag and labelled either "blood and body precautions" or "isolated".

☐ When laying out bodies, all guidelines for using protective equipment and handling contaminated items should be observed.

7. SPECIAL EDUCATION FOR HCWs

☐ Education in caring for patients with any blood-borne infection, including AIDS, is essential for all HCWs.

☐ Refresher courses must be offered at regular intervals to maintain infection control and safe handling procedures.

☐ Any new procedures adopted by a health care facility should be taught as soon as possible in special education sessions.

8. PRECAUTIONS FOR CARDIO PULMONARY RESUSCITATION (CPR) AND CPR TRAINING

Although very small quantities of HIV have been found in saliva, there have been no cases of the virus infection being transmitted through CPR on a person who has AIDS or through contact with a manikin during CPR training.

HCWs who regularly give mouth-to-mouth resuscitation or CPR may protect themselves from a variety of diseases by using a specially designed, disposable, mouthpiece. Health care facilities may choose to keep this disposable, resuscitation equipment at the bedsides of persons with AIDS. However, the risk of infection is so slight that no one should hesitate to give emergency resuscitation without a mouthpiece.

9. WHAT TO DO IN CASE OF NEEDLESTICK INJURY

☐ HCWs should report any accidental injuries or breaks in hygienic technique to their supervisors for appropriate treatment or monitoring.

☐ All incidents should be reported to the employee health service.

☐ The Department of National Health and Welfare is conducting a follow-up study of all HCWs exposed to HIV (by needlestick, by contamination of an open wound, by splash in the eye, or by ingestion). Employee health services can obtain forms from:

The Federal Centre for AIDS
Bureau of Epidemiology and Surveillance
OTTAWA, Ontario K1A 0L2

or from provincial departments of health.
*Note: The Federal Centre for AIDS also has guidelines
for HCWs which are updated on a regular basis.*

AIDS AND YOU

As a private citizen, how can I help in the attack on AIDS?

First, you should be seriously concerned about the AIDS epidemic – not panicked. A healthy and mature attitude toward AIDS will only be developed through your knowledge of the disease and how the virus is transmitted and how it can be prevented. No one need fear AIDS if they follow the guidelines outlined in this book, and you should pass on the information that you have learned. It is misinformation and irrational concerns that create an 'epidemic of fear' and this is almost more dangerous and alarming than the disease itself.

Second, all concerned citizens should be sure that AIDS information is being circulated in their community. If you think your community is not being provided with sufficient information on AIDS, then contact or write your local politicians, or members of parliament and express your concerns. *Remember: An informed community is a healthy and more productive one.*

Third, if you have the time and there is a local AIDS group in your area, volunteer your services. You may be called upon to do anything from stuffing envelopes to assisting persons with AIDS, but whatever efforts you make as a volunteer will be personally gratifying and genuinely appreciated.

Finally, if you have the financial means, consider making a donation to your local AIDS group or PWA (Persons With AIDS) group. These organizations are only partially funded by local, federal and provincial grants, and they count heavily on private and corporate sponsorship for the work that they do. Donations of this nature are also tax deductible.

If you are interested in AIDS research or education, then you might consider making a donation. Contact the Federal Centre for AIDS or the Canadian Public Health Association – their addresses can be found at the back of the book.

Whatever you do to help will be in your interest and that of all Canadians.

The attack on AIDS is everyone's concern. It is an attack on the virus and the epidemic – not on people. Individuals affected by AIDS will need support and understanding, as anyone with a serious health problem.

As a company/corporation, how can we help in the attack on AIDS?

Follow the guidelines described in this book under **AIDS and the Workplace.**

Education and Research are the keys to ultimately defeating AIDS. Take the initiative and be sure your employees are provided with all available information on AIDS. Your local AIDS group and departments of health will provide you with *free* literature.

Become a corporate sponsor for one of the AIDS groups in Canada listed at the back of this book. Your company's resources and/or services could be of genuine assistance.

Consider making a corporate donation to either your local AIDS group, or if you're interested in AIDS research or education in Canada, send your contribution to the Canadian Public Health Association.

Use your corporate influence with local politicians and members of parliament if you feel your community needs more attention to the AIDS epidemic.

Whatever you do to help the fight against AIDS will be in the best interest of yourself, your employees, and that of all Canadians.

If I need more information on AIDS, who should I contact?

Contact any of the AIDS groups or advisory committees listed at the back of this book on pages 131–135, or contact your local health authorities. If you suspect for a moment that you could be an AIDS virus carrier or are suffering from AIDS-related illnesses or symptoms described in this book on page 36, then you are urged to see your doctor.

If I wish to make a contribution to fight AIDS, to whom should I send my cheque?

Your donation would be gratefully received by any of the AIDS groups listed on pages 131–135 (look for the AIDS group in your area).

If you would like to contribute to AIDS research and education, you should mail your cheque to the Canadian Public Health Association.

Do not send cash in the mail.

Index

THE AIDS COMMITTEES,
COMMUNITY GROUPS,
AND ADVISORY BOARDS IN CANADA

CANADIAN PUBLIC HEALTH ASSOCIATION
1565 Carling Avenue, Suite 400
OTTAWA, Ontario K1Z 8R1
(613) 725-3769

FEDERAL CENTRE FOR AIDS
Health Protection Branch, Health and Welfare Canada
301 Elgin Street, 2nd Floor
OTTAWA, Ontario K1A 0L3
(613) 957-1772

BRITISH COLUMBIA MINISTRY OF HEALTH
Vancouver: 872-6652 / Throughout B.C.: 1-800-972-2437

MANITOBA HEALTH DEPARTMENT
AIDS Infoline
Winnipeg 945-AIDS / Throughout Manitoba 1-800-AIDS

NORTHWEST TERRITORIES AIDS PROGRAM
Government of the Northwest Territories
In Yellowknife: 1-403-920-6542

QUEBEC DEPARTMENT OF HEALTH
In Quebec: 1-800-463-5656

ALBERTA COMMUNITY & OCCUPATIONAL HEALTH
In Edmonton: (403) 427-2830
Throughout Alberta: 1-800-772-AIDS

ONTARIO PUBLIC EDUCATION PANEL ON AIDS (OPEPA)

Public Health Branch, 15 Overlea Blvd., 5th Floor
TORONTO, Ontario M4H 1A9
(416) 965-2168 / Toll free: 1-800-268-6066

COMMUNITY AIDS GROUPS

CANADIAN AIDS SOCIETY
10704-108 Street
EDMONTON, Alberta T5H 3A3
(403) 424-4767

AIDS VANCOUVER ISLAND
P.O. Box 845, Station 'E'
Victoria, B.C. V8W 2R9
(604) 384-4554/2366

AIDS VANCOUVER
Box 4991, Main Post Office
VANCOUVER, British Columbia V8B 4A6
OFFICE: 509 - 1033 Davie Street
VANCOUVER, British Columbia V6E 1N4
(604) 687-2437 / AIDS Info. (604) 872-6652

VANCOUVER PWA COALITION
Box 136, 1215 Davie Street
VANCOUVER, British Columbia V6E 1N4
(604) 683-3381

AIDS CALGARY AWARENESS ASSOCIATION
Box 2388, Station M
CALGARY, Alberta T2P 3C1
OFFICE: 223 - 12th Avenue S.W.
CALGARY, Alberta T2R 0G9
(403) 262-2522

AIDS NETWORK OF EDMONTON SOCIETY
10704-108 Street
EDMONTON, Alberta T5J 0M7
(403) 424-4767

AIDS SASKATOON
P.O. Box 4062
SASKATOON, Saskatchewan S7K 4E3
(306) 242-5005 / Toll Free province-wide 1-800-667-6876

AIDS REGINA INC.
Box 3414 REGINA, Saskatchewan S4P 3J8
(306) 522-4522

WINNIPEG GAY COMMUNITY HEALTH CARE, INC.
P.O. Box 3175
WINNIPEG, Manitoba R3C 4E6
OFFICE: The Village Clinic, 709 Corydon Avenue,
WINNIPEG, Manitoba R3M 0W4
(204) 453-0045 / AIDS Info. Line (204) 453-2114

AIDS COMMITTEE OF THUNDER BAY (ACT'B)
19 Regent Street
THUNDER BAY, Ontario P7A 5J5
(807) 345-2315

AIDS COMMITTEE OF WINDSOR
Box 7002
WINDSOR, Ontario N9C 3Y6
(519) 969-0053 / 256-2437

AIDS COMMITTEE OF LONDON
649 Colborne Street
LONDON, Ontario N6A 3Z2
(519) 434-8160

HAMILTON AIDS NETWORK FOR DIALOGUE AND SUPPORT
(HANDS)
P.O. Box 146, Station A
HAMILTON, Ontario L8N 3A2
(416) 528-0854

AIDS COMMITTEE OF TORONTO (ACT)
P.O. Box 55, Station F
TORONTO, Ontario M4Y 3A2
OFFICE: 464 Yonge Street, Suite 202
TORONTO, Ontario M4Y 1G2
(416) 926-1626 / AIDS Info. 1-800-268-6066

AIDS COMMITTEE OF REGIONAL NIAGARA (ACORN)
P.O. Box 61
ST. CATHARINES, Ontario L2R 6R4
(416) 641-8800

AIDS COMMITTEE OF CAMBRIDGE, KITCHENER,
WATERLOO AND AREA
c/o Gordon Youngman, Box 1925
KITCHENER, Ontario N2G 4R4
(519) 576-2127

TORONTO PWA FOUNDATION
Box 1065, Station 'Q'
TORONTO, Ontario M4T 2P2
(416) 927-7644

KINGSTON AIDS PROJECT
Box 2154
KINGSTON, Ontario K7L 5J9
(613) 545-1414 / 549-1232

AIDS COMMITTEE OF OTTAWA
P.O. Box 3043, Station D
OTTAWA, Ontario K1P 6H8
(613) 238-3687

COMITE SIDA-AIDE MONTREAL (C-SAM)
Case postale 98, Station N
MONTREAL, (Quebec) H2X 3M2
OFFICE: 3600 Rue de l'Hotel de Ville
MONTREAL (Quebec)
(514) 282-9888

MONTREAL AIDS RESOURCE COMMITTEE/
ASSOCIATION DES RESSOURCES MONTREALAISES SUR LE
SIDA (MARC-ARMS)
Case postale 1164, Succursale B
MONTREAL, (Quebec) H3G 2N1
(514) 937-7596

MOUVEMENT D'INFORMATION et D'ENTRAIDE dans la lutte
contre le SIDA (MIELS-Quebec) a Quebec
369 Rue St. Jean
QUEBEC, P.Q. G1R 1N8
(418) 687-4310

METRO AREA COMMITTEE ON AIDS (MACAIDS)
P.O. Box 1364, Station M, HALIFAX, Nova Scotia B3J 2X1
(902) 425-4882

NEWFOUNDLAND AND LABRADOR AIDS ASSOCIATION
P.O. Box 1364, Station C, ST. JOHN'S, Newfoundland A1C 5N5
(709) 739-7975

AIDS NEW BRUNSWICK
65 Brunswick St.
FREDERICTON, New Brunswick E3B 1G5

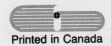
Printed in Canada